D0128723

If This Is Social Studies, Why Isn't It Boring?

If This Is
Social Studies,
Why Isn't It
Boring?

Edited by
Stephanie Steffey
Wendy J. Hood

Stenhouse Publishers
York, Maine

Stenhouse Publishers, 226 York Street, York, Maine 03909

Library of Congress Cataloging-in-Publication Data

If this is social studies, why isn't it boring? / edited by Stephanie
    Steffey and Wendy J. Hood.
        p. cm.
    Includes bibliographical references.
    ISBN 1-57110-003-2
    1. Social sciences—Study and teaching (Elementary)—United
States. I. Steffey, Stephanie, 1947– . II. Hood, Wendy J.
LB1584.I4   1994
327.83'0973—dc20   94–22255
                                                         CIP

Cover and interior design by Maria Szmauz
Cover photograph by Joel Brown

Manufactured in the United States of America on acid-free paper

99   8 7 6 5

Contents

Acknowledgments

AT TIMES, THIS BOOK SEEMED TO BE PROPELLED BY ITS own momentum. There were, however, many people involved in its creation, and we would like to express our gratitude to them. We are grateful to the participants of the Winter 1992 Language and Literacy Workshop in Tucson, Arizona. It was at this workshop that we first explored together the notion of a whole language social studies book. When we shared our idea with other workshop participants, their response was so positive we began immediately to contact potential contributors.

It is to the contributors, all of whom were or are classroom teachers, that we owe an enormous debt. Teachers are hardworking and dedicated people. We asked these teachers to go one step further, to give one more piece of themselves. We asked them to sit down and write out the stories they had to tell. To these teachers we say thank you. Thank you for the initial manuscript drafts, the rewrites and final details. Thank you for your patience and belief in us and your wise words and good humor. Thank you also for striving to meet deadlines and being agreeable to making "just one more change." Most of all, thank you for sharing your stories and your classrooms—without you and your students this book would not be.

We are also enormously grateful to our respective families. To our parents, who supported us with encouragement and pride; to our husbands, who gave us the necessary time and space to work; and to our children, whose patience is attributable to their desire to have the world filled with the kinds of teachers represented here.

ix

We are indebted to Philippa Stratton, our editor at Stenhouse. Philippa received our manuscript with enthusiasm and made the publishing process as easy as possible.

We have tried to retain the story and the voice of each contributor. Final responsibility for the book's content, however, rests with us. Our hope is that, for some number of teachers, this book will have a profound influence on their teaching of social studies. And, like the contributors to this book, those who are influenced will write their stories, and those they influence will write their stories, until there is but one universal story.

About the Authors

JANET ALLEN was a secondary teacher of English/Reading for twenty years and a Milken National Educator Award recipient for literacy work with at-risk students. She is currently a Professor of English Education at the University of Central Florida.

HEATHER BLAIR is currently a doctoral candidate in the Department of Language, Reading, and Culture at the University of Arizona. Formerly a middle and secondary school teacher, she has also taught for the Saskatchewan Urban Native Teacher Education Program at the University of Saskatchewan.

BRENDA BROWN has been an elementary school teacher for seven years in the ABC Unified School District in Cerritos, California. Presently she teaches fourth grade and is particularly interested in the development of democratic classrooms.

ROBIN CAMPBELL is Professor of Primary Education at the University of Hertfordshire in England. His previous roles as a primary school teacher and headteacher are reflected in his research interests of teachers and children working together in literacy activities. His two most recent books are *Reading Together* and *Reading Real Books*, both published by Open University Press.

KATHLEEN CRAWFORD was a teacher at Maldonado Elementary School in Tucson Unified School District, Tucson, Arizona, where she taught first, second, and fourth grades. She is currently a full-time doctoral student in the Department of Language, Reading, and Culture at the University of Arizona, where she teaches children's literature to pre-service teachers.

MARGARET FERGUSON is a multi-age (ages six through eight) teacher at Corbett Elementary School in Tucson Unified School District, Tucson, Arizona. She previously taught first grade and recently completed a masters degree in Language, Reading, and Culture at the University of Arizona.

PAUL FISHER is Director of the Tucson Pima Arts Council and has brought his expertise and collaboration to upper-grade classrooms in Tucson, Arizona.

MEEGAN I. GLINER recently completed the multiple subject (elementary education) credential program at San Jose State University, San Jose, California. She teaches a multi-grade (ages eleven through fourteen) self-contained class in the Franklin-McKinley School District in San Jose.

SHEILA HOFSTEDT is an upper-grade teacher for the Albuquerque Public Schools in New Mexico. She enjoys watching U.S. history come alive for students. During her time away from the classroom she leads volunteer trips to Tonga, Mexico, and other developing countries.

WENDY J. HOOD teaches kindergarten in the Tucson Unified School District, Tucson, Arizona. She has taught second and third grade and is the coeditor of *The Whole Language Evaluation Book* and *Organizing for Whole Language*, both published by Heinemann.

LESLIE KAHN is a multi-age (ages nine through eleven) teacher at Robbins Elementary School in the Tucson Unified

School District, Tucson, Arizona. She invites members of the community to collaborate with her students in her literature and inquiry based classroom.

SANDY KASER teaches fifth grade in the Tucson Unified School District, Tucson, Arizona. Through the graduate courses she has taken at the University of Arizona, she has been working towards a literature- and inquiry-based classroom.

GLORIA KAUFFMAN currently teaches in a multi-age primary classroom (ages six through nine) at Maldonado Elementary School in Tucson Unified School District, Tucson, Arizona. Previously she taught fourth grade at Maldonado and moved with her students to fifth grade. Before moving to Tucson, she taught first through third grade in Goshen, Indiana.

JULIE LAIRD teaches kindergarten and Reading Recovery at Cragin Elementary School in Tucson Unified School District, Tucson, Arizona. She is a doctoral student in the Department of Language, Reading, and Culture at the University of Arizona.

DIANA MAZZUCHI has been a classroom teacher for twenty-four years. Presently, she is team teaching in a primary multi-age (ages six through nine) classroom at Academy School in Brattleboro, Vermont. Diana is a frequent presenter at national workshops and conferences on whole language and multi-age teaching.

JANET NELSON has been a primary special education teacher of mildly to moderately intellectually challenged, autistic, and language-disordered students for the past fifteen years. She resides in Beaverton, Oregon, and her interest in social studies and whole language has involved her in a Kyotaru fellowship to Japan, travel to Africa, and observation of classrooms in Australia and New Zealand.

ELIZABETH NOLL, a doctoral candidate in the Department of Language, Reading, and Culture at the University of Arizona, was a teacher of sixth and seventh grade for fifteen years. She has also taught at the university level and served as a consultant to classroom teachers and administrators.

DANA PITT is a practicing attorney in Tucson, Arizona. She is currently enrolled as a graduate student in the Department of Language, Reading, and Culture at the University of Arizona.

RUTH J. SÁEZ VEGA is an assistant professor at the University of Puerto Rico, where she has taught kindergarten at the laboratory school and undergraduate courses in the areas of early childhood and literacy. Her teaching experience includes preschool and first and fourth grade. Currently she is a doctoral candidate in the program of Language, Reading, and Culture at the University of Arizona.

JEAN SCHROEDER teaches a multi-age primary classroom (ages six through nine) at Cragin Elementary School in Tucson Unified School District, Tucson, Arizona. She is a doctoral student in the Department of Language, Reading, and Culture at the University of Arizona.

MARNI SCHWARTZ taught language arts and social studies in Niskayuna, New York for over sixteen years. Currently she is a storyteller in schools, libraries, and museums, and for community organizations. She works with teachers in classrooms and college classes, and at conferences. She coedited *Give a Listen: Stories of Storytelling in Schools,* which will be published by NCTE in 1994.

KATHY G. SHORT is Associate Professor in the Department of Language, Reading, and Culture at the University of Arizona. She teaches courses on children's literature, the integration of literature into the curriculum, and collaborative environments that support the inquiry of teachers and students.

SUZANNE SOOHOO is Assistant Professor in the School of Education at Chapman University, Orange, California. She teaches courses on teaching and learning, school leadership, and multicultural education.

STEPHANIE STEFFEY currently divides her time between teaching multi-age primary (ages six through eight) in the Santa Clara Unified School District and teaching college courses in the Division of Teacher Education at San Jose State University, San Jose, California. She previously taught kindergarten for eight years.

WENDY J. HOOD

Introduction

IN THE MUSHROOMING FIELD OF BOOKS ON ALL ASPECTS
of whole language education, it seems odd that there are so few
books about social studies in the whole language classroom.
When Stephanie Steffey and I first approached Philippa Stratton
about our idea for this book, she responded enthusiastically.
There had been some attempts to create whole language social
studies books in the past. However, those written by social
studies specialists were criticized by whole language practitioners as not being holistic enough, while those written from a
whole language perspective were criticized by the social studies
people as lacking in social studies theory.

Most whole language teachers can recite lists of researchers
in whole language. They quote Ken or Yetta Goodman easily
when talking of reading. Names like Don Graves, Nancie
Atwell, and Lucy Calkins come up often as they discuss writing. At a recent interview for a whole language classroom posi-
tion, every applicant cited Marilyn Burns when talking about
mathematics. Today's whole language teachers readily name
authors and illustrators of children's fiction and poetry. It is less
likely that they can name writers of social studies theory—John
Jarolimek or James Banks, for example—or authors of children's
nonfiction, such as Milton Meltzer or Aliki. These educators do
not neglect social studies education in their classrooms. Many,
like the authors of this book, are skilled practitioners who bring
students to new understandings in all the social studies disciplines. Why is it, then, that such knowledgeable professionals
appear to lack scholarly expertise in this field?

Perhaps it is because these teachers had no required social
studies method courses in their teacher preparation programs.
Although this is changing, in most states in the United States, a
minimal amount of undergraduate coursework in U.S. history
and social sciences and a test on the local state constitution are
still sufficient qualifications for elementary and middle school
teachers of social studies (Ochoa 1981).

Perhaps it is because of the ongoing argument between
those who contend that social studies is an integration of all the
social sciences and those who say that history, geography, and
so on require separate attention—a "whole versus part" argument familiar to many whole language teachers. Inherent in
that argument as it pertains to social studies are issues relating
to authority, inquiry, resources, and teaching (Broadhead and
Burnett 1955). To better understand the argument, one must
understand the history of social studies.

Social Studies: A Brief History 1

"Social studies" as a term entered the educational jargon in 1916. In 1915 and 1916, Arthur William Dunn edited two documents, *Civic Education in Elementary Schools as Illustrated in Indianapolis* and *The Social Studies in Secondary Education: Report of the Committee on Social Studies of the Commission on the Reorganization of Secondary Education of the National Education Association.* These outlined what remains a basic structure for social studies today: kindergartners study self and school; first grade, families; second grade, neighborhood; and so on, with good citizenship a major goal for all grades (Morrissett 1981). Throughout the twentieth century, the pendulum has swung back and forth, with social studies educators or society at large placing various pressures on classroom teachers.

The progressive education movement of the early part of this century encouraged teachers to "engage learners in problem solving, in an analysis of social issues, in thinking, and in reasoning" (Jarolimek 1981, p. 6). During this time teachers were encouraged to integrate all the social science disciplines into social studies and also to integrate other curricular areas into social studies!

Between 1915 and the end of World War II, many specific requirements were placed on classroom teachers. For example, during the First World War, *Lessons in Community and National Life* were implemented in the classroom to help teach the need for conservation, much like the "Reduce, Reuse, Recycle" programs of today. In the early 1920s a social studies curriculum was developed by a superintendent that chronologically, beginning with Jesus Christ, taught grade-five children social studies facts that he and his group of researchers believed were important. In 1943 a national outcry for more specific teaching of history resulted when the *New York Times* published a series of articles announcing the "historical illiteracy" of American students, similar to the recent outcry over students' alleged lack of geographical knowledge (Davis 1981).

Following the Second World War, the influence of progressive education was still felt in most classrooms. According to Jarolimek, "social studies served as the 'integrating center' of the curriculum. Reading, language arts, arithmetic, science, health, music, drama, and art were often planned around and related to the comprehensive 'units' that were the organizing frameworks anchored in social studies. The dominant disciplines were history and geography, although there was a tendency to integrate the two subjects and to blur the boundaries between them. Educators stress the importance of 'pupil-involving learning activities'," (1981, p. 6). It was during this time that what is now called multicultural education was introduced.

McCarthyism and other pressures of the 1950s saw many teachers shy away from anything other than approved textbooks and "acceptable" facts. Broadhead and Burnett discussed this issue at length in their 1955 article "Areas of Change and Controversy." "The question of what constitutes the proper and advisable boundaries of inquiry within social studies classrooms," they wrote, "has become increasingly controversial. . . . Stemming from the international tensions characterizing the post-war period have been questions of indoctrination, propaganda, and subversion, repercussions from which have been felt in classrooms across the nation. Closely related to the boundaries of inquiry has been the question of methods of inquiry" (p. 32). During that era teaching methods and resources were severely limited; even textbooks were suspected of being subversive. "These conditions have given rise to what amounts to self-censorship on the part of teachers" (Broadhead and Burnett 1955, p. 32).

In the post-Sputnik era of the late 1950s, the public demanded change. Monies were poured into universities and foundations for the development of "New Social Studies" materials. By the late 1960s, relevance had become a key word. "Presentism was in; historical studies were out" (Jarolimek 1981, p. 10).

The "back to basics" movement in the 1970s and an increasing emphasis on standardized tests were the next trends to affect the teaching of social studies. Jarolimek asserts, "Recent national surveys and studies on the status of social studies indicate that the 'back to basics' movement has affected social studies, but often in an adverse way. For example, elementary school teachers are devoting less instructional time to social studies in order to give more attention to reading, writing, and arithmetic. The increased use of competency examinations as a requirement for high school graduation has also led schools to emphasize those skills, topics, and subjects that are tested" (1981, p. 13).

Throughout this century, American social studies educators have repeated their call for change in social studies education. In his 1975 text, *Teaching Strategies for Ethnic Studies*, James

Banks called for a clarification of goals and a change of teaching strategies in reference to multicultural education: "Unless a sound rationale for ethnic studies programs can be stated and new approaches to the teaching of ethnic studies implemented, students will get just as sick and tired of ethnic content as they have become with White chauvinistic schoolbook history. . . . Without both new goals and novel strategies, ethnic studies will become just another fleeting fad. Isolated facts about Crispus Attucks and Crazy Horse do not stimulate the intellect any more than isolated facts about Thomas Jefferson and Abraham Lincoln." Ethnic studies did pass from view for a while for exactly the reason Banks stated so well: "Many teachers who teach ethnic studies programs use new materials but traditional strategies because multiethnic materials, although necessary for sound social studies programs, do not in themselves solve the classroom teacher's pedagogical problems" (p. 28).

Pedagogical problems! Contemporary whole language teachers now have well-thought-out philosophies of education. They have rejected basal readers and simplified textbooks. In doing so, they have also rejected most social studies texts and, for a time, the field of social studies as a whole.

Contemporary whole language teachers have rejected the use of textbooks that proceed country by country and ask seventh graders such questions as "What are three ways of showing scale on a map?" or "Who was the French explorer who traveled the St. Lawrence River?" They reject programs with worksheets that depict both stretched animal hides and bricks and that ask second graders to mark the *one* thing "Indians made their homes from." They reject cutesy activities such as growing three sweet potatoes and naming them George, Washington, and Carver.

Other Futures

In 1981, Morrissett asked, "Are other futures possible? . . . Is it not possible that some radical changes in the old order of things are indicated—changes in the teacher-centered, textbook-dominated, thirty-students-in-a-box way of doing things?" (p. 58).

Today's whole language teachers have made the changes necessary for implementation of a different kind of curriculum. They have once again moved away from "teacher-proof" texts and fragmented days to child-centered classrooms and integrated curricula. As Morrissett suggests, they have broken away from the "dominant curriculum pattern" of the last half century. As Banks proposed, they have made that pedagogical shift. Now they are also ready to teach a new kind of social studies.

They've come back to the teaching of social studies through a number of avenues. The authors in this book demonstrate this variety. Few set out initially to change their social studies instruction, but they did set out to change instruction. None perceive themselves as social studies experts, yet all have found a need to come back to social studies education, to a different kind of social studies education.

Elizabeth Noll came back because "I wanted [students] to make personal connections with their learning and to approach it from a number of perspectives." Sandy Kaser was driven by her concern that her students "were not reading books." She "began to wonder: if I provided more support in the classroom to help these students understand their roots and therefore understand themselves, would this invite connections to literature and one another?" Within their classrooms, Suzanne SooHoo and Brenda Brown were faced with "a diversity of customs and cultures." Their "challenge was to build a classroom community in which individual strengths and differences were respected and regularly celebrated." Kathleen Crawford, Margaret Ferguson, Gloria Kauffman, Julie Laird, Jean Shroeder, and Kathy G. Short "wanted our students not only to be problem-solvers but to become problem-posers." Heather Blair was working through an interactive model of instruction with "a sharing of knowledge, decision making, power, and voice." She ponders, "What does voice mean for indigenous people?" Ruth Sáez Vega was confronted with a group of five-year-olds concerned about a present-day war. When Robin Campbell observed that "children try to read material other than stories," he raised a question: How might children be assisted in their understanding of expository books? And Marni Schwartz returned to social studies through her experiences as a storyteller.

The Social Sciences

The authors have not only rediscovered social studies education in general, they have also found themselves exploring the many disciplines of the social sciences that combine to make social studies. The social sciences—sociology, political science, anthropology, psychology, geography, economics, and history—are disciplines that have been developed into separate areas for university research and teaching. Although the authors don't use the labels, each of the social sciences is visible in each classroom represented in this book. The issues of the disciplines are visible, the content of the disciplines is visible, and the questions central to each discipline are central in these classrooms.

These disciplines are faced in new ways, and for new purposes. They are integrated in whole language classrooms as they are integrated in life. Each author began with a focus on one or more specific social science disciplines. In every case, however, while the studies began in one discipline, they branched out or melted into one or more of the others. Such is the nature of the social sciences; such is the nature of the whole language classroom.

SOCIOLOGY: THE STUDY OF HUMAN SOCIETY AND SOCIAL RELATIONS, ORGANIZATION, AND CHANGE

Sociology in the whole language classroom is taught on many levels. On one level, as students learn how a society functions or changes, they learn about sociology. On another, the students interact in social ways, in groupings of various sizes, to achieve a common goal. On this level, the classroom becomes the society. Taken a step further, participants enter into discussion about the group process, which leads them to deeper understandings of how society works.

For Leslie Kahn, Paul Fisher, and Dana Pitt, sociology was defined as a key goal. As part of the study of the Holocaust, Kahn wanted her students "to become aware of themselves as members of a community (local, national, global) in which they have both responsibility and a voice." The Holocaust raised many sociological issues for their students. They began to ask tough moral questions, first of others ("Why would anyone want to be a Nazi?" "Why would people want to kill other people?"), then of themselves ("It's like you kind of want to do it but you know you shouldn't, and then. . . ").

Many of the teachers use a variety of grouping strategies to support student learning. For some, like Elizabeth Noll, grouping is incidental to the process, a classroom reflecting society. "I asked the students to meet in small groups and share. . . . The students were familiar with brainstorming. . . . I set aside time daily for the groups to browse and read the library books. . . . Individual students and groups recorded their own comings and goings." Sandy Kaser's students are also grouped for learning. "I arranged these materials in baskets and rotated them through small groups of children for browsing. . . . Each group of students chose one set of books to reread and to discuss." Though her groupings also appear second nature, Kaser remains aware of a need to communicate expectations. "To demonstrate good sharing and discussion, I also read aloud to the students and encouraged responses in whole class discussion." Sheila Hofstedt's students had less experience working in groups. For them, it was as important to learn how to work in a group as it was to learn with the group. "I felt it was important for there to be specific guidelines for behavior and expectations within the literature groups. This was the first experience working in this way for many of the students."

For Suzanne SooHoo and Brenda Brown, sociology is the framework. They established a classroom where class meetings are convened once a week. The class comes together as a whole to work out problems and concerns. In the beginning, the teachers help raise sociological issues to a cognitive level. They deal with such concerns as how to get along in groups and how the class can function as a whole. Later on, the students focus on broader social issues that reach outside the class setting.

POLITICAL SCIENCE: THE STUDY OF THE PRINCIPLES, ORGANIZATION, AND METHODS OF GOVERNMENT

Understanding political science issues was one of Sheila Hofstedt's goals. "I wanted my students to realize that war, like life, is not a black and white issue, and that there are often more than two sides to any issue." Developing an understanding of multiple perspectives was also important to Elizabeth Noll. "My goal was to have the students be able to compare viewpoints from multiple sources of information, the textbook being only one source."

My own students, in our studies together, discovered the discipline of political science. Issues of power and changing laws became important in what I had seen as an anthropological study of Native American cultures. "Immediately they recognized many similarities between George Bush's campaign promises and ones made by Andrew Johnson in his reelection campaign." When my students learned of Martin Luther King, Jr., and Rosa Parks, they kept returning to the idea that "Martin Luther King changed laws." And when they saw that "when Momma Parks sat down, the whole world stood up!" they began to wonder if kids could make that kind of change as well.

Five-year-olds, such as the ones in Ruth Sáez Vega's class, can also explore political science. They tried to reason through a war. "Yo no entiendo porqué Hussein y Bush tienen que pelear" (I don't understand why Hussein and Bush have to fight).

ANTHROPOLOGY: THE STUDY OF PEOPLE; THEIR VARIETY, PHYSICAL AND CULTURAL CHARACTERISTICS, DISTRIBUTION, CUSTOMS, AND SOCIAL RELATIONSHIPS

Anthropology is a focus for both Sandy Kaser and Heather Blair. Sandy explains, "I considered my own classroom, where the students are Native American, African American, Mexican American, and European American. . . . Each ethnic group tended to be studied in isolation. . . . Ethnicity appeared to be static and uniform rather than a dynamic feature of the living children in the room. I could not recall the students ever making a personal response to any of these lessons. . . . I developed plans for a cross-curricular, literature-based family studies inquiry."

The face-to-face interview, a major anthropological tool, became important for many of our authors. Janet Allen began by trying to ease her students into a liking for history and wound up taking them into the area of anthropology as well. "I wanted history to become real for them. . . . I asked each of the students to interview a family member or acquaintance who had lived during the Depression." When she became aware that her students were not yet ready to be anthropologists, "We spent the next day brainstorming some sample interview questions. . . . After a day of practicing with tape recorders as we interviewed each other in class, the students were ready."

Diana Mazzuchi's students became so interested in the businesses in the area they were mapping, they wanted to learn more. "It became obvious that the answer to the question 'How will we find out?' could not be found in books. We would have to go directly to the [primary] source[s]." Like Allen's students, Mazzuchi's spent time learning how to be anthropologists before heading out into the field.

PSYCHOLOGY: THE STUDY OF ANIMAL AND HUMAN BEHAVIOR, DEALING WITH THE MIND AND THE EMOTIONS

Heather Blair reminds us of the importance of psychology. "It has been suggested that children of color drop out of school because school is not related to their lives. . . . We need to reexamine not only the process of teaching and learning but the content as well. . . . Ask yourselves the following questions: What matters to these kids? What is going on in their lives? What is bothering them? What turns them on?"

For Leslie Kahn, Paul Fisher, and Dana Pitt, the discipline of psychology became important when some students seemed to be apathetic. Leslie "particularly challenged kids who attempted to disengage from the conversation with 'I don't care' comments. . . . While talking about the 'no Jews allowed' rule" she made the situation more realistic to a child who then replied, "I'd be mad."

My students also led us into psychology. In their study of slavery, they became appalled by certain conditions. Two issues were repeated frequently in their writing: the lack of basic necessities and the frequent physical abuse. Daniel and Jeff summed up the class's concern: "Slaves wore rags when they were adults and when they were kids. If they were a girl, they wore a shirt. Boys wore pants. They had to sleep on boards. Slaves got whipped a lot if they broke something, like a branch on a cotton plant, or tried to escape. If the slaves took a breath they'd get whipped. They never got any fun at all."

GEOGRAPHY: THE STUDY OF THE SURFACE OF THE EARTH, ITS DIVISION INTO NATURAL CONTINENTS AND POLITICAL REGIONS, AND THE CLIMATE, PLANTS, INHABITANTS, AND RESOURCES OF THOSE DIVISIONS

Diana Mazzuchi's original plan called for her students to begin a study by mapping the neighborhood. But they remained involved in studying cartography long past her initial expectations. "Suddenly maps of all kinds began appearing in the classroom. Katie brought in a map of Paris that had been hanging in her home for years, but that she had never paid any attention to."

Many of the authors of this book found opportunities for their students to turn to maps. For others, students raised the geographical issues. Meegan Gliner's students wanted to know how Native Americans distinguished between what land belonged to which tribe. Some of Janet Allen's students chose to map the travels of characters from an important book.

One map sent Sandy Kaser's class "spiraling off from my original plan for about six weeks." One student drew "a rough map of her neighborhood and highlighted the places that were of importance to her."

Geography is a recurrent theme with Janet Nelson's exceptional children, even though their topic of study is a restaurant. They study school landmarks when deciding where to locate their restaurant. They create maps as part of their advertising. And the question "How can we get more food?" leads them to revisit their previous study of farms where they learned how food goes from farm to table.

ECONOMICS: THE STUDY OF THE PRODUCTION, DISTRIBUTION, AND CONSUMPTION OF WEALTH, WITH THE RELATED ISSUES OF LABOR, FINANCE, AND TAXES

"Slaves were doing all the work so the white plantation owners would get the money" was what my students Daniel and Jeff wrote in their piece on slaves. In a report on cotton, Josh and Santiago noted, "A long time ago, before the Civil War, black slaves used to grow the cotton. They used to work on it every day. Now the farmers have to pay people to do the work of growing cotton." The economics of slavery was clear to my students. It brought out discussions about chores and allowance!

Janet Allen's students easily understood the economics of the Depression. "I also knew that students would be able to understand the similarity between the plight of the farms in the 1930s and the problems farmers were experiencing in northern Maine during the 1980s." Through skillful questioning, Janet Nelson leads her young learners to explore consumer economics: "What will happen when all the food is given out and eaten up? How can we get more food?"

HISTORY: THE SYSTEMATIC STUDY OF THE PAST; THE RECORDING, ANALYZING, CORRELATING, AND EXPLAINING OF PAST EVENTS

Rather than let "I hate history" comments float about her classroom, Janet Allen addressed history through her field of English education. "It occurred to me that a young adult book I had recently read . . . would be a wonderful way of putting the people back into history. This book was filled with historical information."

Robin Campbell points out that history may be introduced in many ways. A teacher need not go into great detail. "I'm going to read to you about what happened a long time ago" can be a good way to start. A bit of comparison between then and now ("There's still a road . . . but there isn't a baker's shop") may be sufficient.

Meegan Gliner's students took an historical perspective as they investigated Native American peoples. When brainstorming, they only raised questions about issues of indigenous cultures of the *past*. Many peoples have contemporary cultures as well as histories. With gentle guidance, the history of a people may be brought into the present so that students do not believe indigenous peoples to be anachronisms. As stated so well by Kathleen Crawford et al., we have "come to see history as a process."

For the little ones in the class Campbell describes, for the young men and women Allen worked with, as for all the students represented in this book, history has become real in many ways. They see themselves as a part of history, not history as apart from them. For Marni Schwartz it became very personal. As she researched the history of Martin Luther King, Jr., she found strong parallels to her own personal history. She draws connections that propel her to further investigations and explorations. "As I shared both Martin's and my stories, my students began to open up about the moments when they'd witnessed or felt the sting of stereotyping. . . . Martin's story was now our story."

As I read Schwartz's article, Martin's story became mine as well. Throughout his life, Martin Luther King, Jr., interacted with wise teachers. He was encouraged as a thinker to question, to seek knowledge. "His teachers, readings, and further studies . . . contributed to Martin's growth as a thinker and speaker." Such is the nature of whole language!

Thinkers and doers. That is what whole language teachers seek to develop, what social studies educators have always sought. And a new pedagogy. These concepts aren't new. Teachers of the 1920s integrated curriculum; teachers of the 1940s believed in inquiry. The challenges have also been there all along—the demand for the teaching of specific facts, the public outcry over the teaching of controversial issues or critical thinking. What is perhaps new is a unifying philosophical understanding. The authors of this book have returned to social studies because each discovered the need was there. Within their theoretical frame-work, they sought stronger foundations. They wanted students to be involved in their own learning, to be responsible for their own learning, to discover the power of language and its influence, and to be knowledgeable, democratic decision-makers. They discovered, as Kelley describes, that "it is the plain duty of every teacher to abandon the notion that it is his function to delimit learning, and to see that he must help those whom he guides to examine freely and courageously any part of the world of human knowledge that he may come upon" (1955; p. 70). The authors of this book sought change, lasting change, for their students, for themselves, and for their profession. "The teacher then becomes the facilitator of learning and a defender of freedom. This is a fine role for anyone teaching in a democracy" (Kelley 1955, p. 70).

Lasting Change

It was 1981 when Morrissett wrote, "There is no assurance that such changes will be made in the near future." He also set out six "needs and directions for change, beyond a conviction that substantial change is necessary and possible" (1981, p. 58):

1. Freeing teachers from their confining responsibility for controlling and safeguarding every action and every minute of students' learning experiences.
2. Putting more responsibility on students for their own and each others' learning.
3. Shifting the major learning activities from the passive to the active mode; more doing, less listening.

4. Moving a substantial proportion of educational activities out of the classroom and into the library, the school, and the community.
5. Broadening the methods of evaluating student accomplishments, so that grades are not tied so closely to the authority of the teacher and textbook.
6. Broadening the tools of learning beyond the textbook.

These six conditions, set forth by Morrissett, are met and exceeded in the classrooms we visit in this book. They are embedded throughout the stories. The change in pedagogy that preceded our return to social studies we hope will affect the pedagogy of other educators, resulting in lasting change in social studies education.

You are invited to share, and to question, the experiences we have had discovering successful ways to implement change and rediscovering social studies from a whole language perspective. Such is the nature of whole language; such is the nature of learning.

JANET ALLEN

If This Is History, Why Isn't It Boring?

As MY HIGH SCHOOL STUDENTS GATHERED THEIR belongings to go to their next class, I was once again struck by how much they hated to leave my English class and go to history class. Perhaps they saw English as the lesser of two evils, but my sense was that they were experiencing many of my memories of U.S. History class fifteen years before—names and dates, worksheets, and end-of-chapter questions. Although many teachers had stopped listening to these students' complaints, over the past few years I had become increasingly concerned about the way my General English III students felt about their required General U.S. History class. For one thing, since they stayed in my class for two years, I had to listen to their problems more than other teachers. Not only did I listen to their grumbling while they were taking U.S. History as juniors, but I had to continue listening to many of them the following year as June approached and they still needed to make up their missing U.S. History credit in order to graduate. Over time, my class had become the place where students received help with all kinds of problems, both academic and personal, so I knew that if these students were going to get help with history, it would probably happen in my classroom. I also knew that I didn't want to do anything that might disturb the delicate balance of success I had achieved with these students by combining periods of reading aloud with independent reading, writing, and research. I knew that it was important, especially for these uninterested students, to find a way to combine the successful elements of our class and still develop the background knowledge they needed to make history become relevant and meaningful in their lives.

They were not easy students to teach. Having suffered through two years of high school, these students were victims of tracking at its worst. For reasons as diverse as poor attitude, literacy problems, lack of parent involvement, pregnancy, and other social problems, they found their mornings filled with one required "general" class after another. After lunch, most of them went on to vocational courses they had chosen. I often felt exhausted when they left my classroom. It was not because they were discipline problems, but because they seemed so apathetic. Even on days when they were excited about what we were doing in English, as the clock moved closer to 10:00 A.M., I began hearing the common litany of complaints, both from those who had been in History during first period and those who were on the way to History after our English class. As a result, the final moments of our time together were not spent with positive talk about the great book we were reading; rather, it was spent discussing their dislike of history, which transferred to a dislike of the bigger picture—school.

"I hate history."

"Why is it required anyway? Who cares about all that stupid stuff?"

"I wonder if I'd get caught if I skipped?"

"If you thought it was boring yesterday, wait until you see the pile of stupid worksheets we had to do today."

"Gimme your answers to the questions and then I can just sleep. He'll never know the difference."

As much as I wanted to support my colleagues, there was little I could say that could contradict the students' complaints. I remembered my years in a college preparatory U.S. History class, memorizing names, dates, generals, and battles. I, who loved school, wasn't even interested! It had all seemed so lifeless, so mechanical. I wondered what kind of people found history exciting. I compared learning history to my English classes. How could people prefer reading dry historical texts when they could spend their reading time with memorable characters like George and Lennie, Lady Macbeth, and Old Yeller?

Fortunately, for me and my students, I also remembered how my hatred of history had changed into fascination. Recently, I had begun reading both adult and young adult historical fiction. These books had taken all the lifeless names and dates and made them come alive for me. When I began sharing these books with my students in English class, I knew I had found a way to help all of us see the human side of history—the missing piece in their history class and their textbooks.

The Human Factor

Having to learn names, dates, generals, and battles was as true for these students in the 1980s as it was for me in the late 1960s. As an adult, when I first read Jean Fritz's autobiography, *Homesick*, I was struck by her description of American history textbooks:

I skimmed through the pages, but I couldn't find any mention of people at all. There was talk about dates and square miles and cultivation and population growth and immigration and the Western movement, but it was as if the forests had lain down and given way to farmland without anyone being brave or scared or tired or sad, without babies being born, without people dying. (1982, p. 153)

For Jean Fritz, as for me as a history student, it was the people who were missing. It was the people who were missing for my students as well. Since they were currently completing worksheets on World War I, I knew that they soon would be studying the Great Depression. It occurred to me that a young adult book I had recently read, *No Promises in the Wind* (Hunt 1970), would be a wonderful way of putting the people back into history. This book was filled with historical information about the Depression, but the events unfolded through the eyes of two characters, Josh and Joey. During the worst year of the Depression, Josh, Joey, and Howie leave home in a search for food and money. On the first day of their trip Howie is killed, leaving Josh and Joey alone to learn about life and the times in which they were living. From my perspective as an English teacher, the book combined adventure with the universal literary and life theme that one must leave home in order to return later with new insights. Josh and Joey's story had the added bonus of taking place in an historical setting the students would soon be studying. So, in our General English class, we began our search for the people in history with Irene Hunt's *No Promises in the Wind*.

Making Connections

From my brush with learning theorists in my undergraduate education courses, I knew that one of the surest ways to help children make new information meaningful is to connect the new information to their lives; therefore, before starting *No Promises in the Wind*, we began our unit with three journal prompts:

1. If I could have or do anything, my impossible dream would be. . . .
2. A time when I planned something and was disappointed. . . .
3. A time in my life when I've been lonely. . . .

Some students, like Tony, wrote of impossible dreams: "I would really love to spend the rest of my life out in the wild—hunting, trapping, and fishing." Most, however, wrote about luxurious cars and homes, dream jobs and great-looking boyfriends and girlfriends. I wondered how they would feel as they revisited these prompts after our common reading, but for the time being I left their combined "wish lists" posted on a wall. After all, Charlotte Huck has reminded us that "literature has the power to take us out of ourselves and return us to ourselves, a changed self" (1987, pp. 69–71).

After our writing and discussions of dreams, disappointment, and loneliness, I set the stage for our class reading of *No Promises in the Wind* by having the students write and talk about conflict. In the book, the conflicts between Josh and his father actually lead to Josh and Joey leaving home; that pattern then repeats itself in the interactions between Josh and his younger brother, Joey. We read Steinbeck's "Flight" and "The Origin of

Armstrong, W. H. 1972. *Sounder*. New York: Harper Trophy.

Cormier, R. 1980. *8 Plus 1*. New York: Bantam.

Lyon, G. E. 1988. *Borrowed Children*. New York: Bantam.

Matthews, A. 1985. *Journey of Natty Gann*. New York: Pocket Books.

Mazer, H. 1986. *The Cave under the City*. New York: Thomas Y. Crowell.

Medearis, A. S. 1990. *Picking Peas for a Penny*. New York: Scholastic.

Peck, R. N. 1972. *A Day No Pigs Would Die*. New York: Dell.

Steinbeck, J. 1937. *Of Mice and Men*. New York: Bantam.

Taylor, M. 1976. *Roll of Thunder, Hear My Cry*. New York: Bantam.

———. 1981. *Song of the Trees*. New York: Bantam.

———. 1989. *The Friendship and the Gold Cadillac*. New York: Bantam-Skylark.

———. 1990. *Mississippi Bridge*. New York: Bantam-Skylark.

Figure 1–1
Supplementary Readings Related to the Depression Era

Tularecito" and examined the ways the characters in those short stories resolved conflict in their lives. We read, wrote, and talked about the ways individuals get into conflict and the ways in which they explore their options. These activities activated a wealth of personal experience, for most of my students lived their lives in almost constant conflict. Finally, after two weeks of exploring other books (Figure 1–1), the world, and their lives, it was time to begin our reading of the novel.

The Power of Literature

I began reading aloud *No Promises in the Wind* just as the cold, rainy, fall days typical of northern Maine had begun. Students could immediately sympathize with Josh's discomfort as the book began:

> I reached out to the bedside table, stopped the alarm, snapped on the shaded study lamp, and lay back on my pillow. The chill of early October had sharpened during the night, and the discomfort of being cold together with too few hours of sleep made me irritable and moody. (7)

These students had just returned from spending four weeks out of school for our annual potato harvest break. Early, cold mornings were definitely familiar to them. They empathized with Josh from the start.

Each day as I read *No Promises in the Wind* aloud to the students, they became more involved in the lives of Josh, Howie, and Joey. They also became more aware of how the Great Depression affected the boys personally. The Great Depression was no longer just a set of dates; rather, it was the cause of the conflicts in Josh and Joey's families. The students could easily see how the lack of work and food led to constant conflicts and eventually the decision the boys made to leave home. As I read the book to the class, we raised questions and made predictions about the story. We compared and contrasted what we were reading with the social studies textbook. Students said they learned more from the novel because it gave them real people to connect the facts and dates to. As we read, we kept a class list of people and events we needed to know more about.

By the time we reached Chapter 8, I felt students had generated enough interest in the historical and social background to be interested in two filmstrips: *The Reckless Years: 1919–1929* and *The Great Depression: 1929–1939*. After watching these two filmstrips and looking at the extensive class list we had generated, we decided to write our own history reference book to accompany the novel. Students drew upon history textbooks, library references, and family members to gather information. Students also identified something in the time period that interested them and engaged in more in-depth research. Eventually our history reference book, *The 30's/The 80's: People Respond to the Times*, included the following topics:

Black Thursday
Warren G. Harding
Albert B. Fall (Teapot Dome Scandal)
Billy Sunday
Clarence Darrow, Scopes Trial
Prohibition and "Rum Runners"
Al Capone
St. Valentine's Day Massacre
Jazz, ragtime, the Charleston
Louis Armstrong, Mae West, Jack Benny, Benny Goodman
The invention of the radio
Amos and Andy, Rudy Vallee, Bing Crosby
Babe Ruth, Knute Rockne, Red Grange
Silent movies, Gloria Swanson, Rudolph Valentino
Charlie Chaplin, Al Jolson
Charles Lindbergh
Sacco and Vanzetti
Calvin Coolidge
F. Scott Fitzgerald, Sinclair Lewis, Ernest Hemingway
Herbert Hoover, "Hoovervilles," Hoover blankets
The New Deal: CCC, TVA
The origin of the Monopoly game
The Bonus March, the Hunger March

Going Outside
the Classroom

The students were proud of their publication, and I was excited about their involvement in both the novel and the related research. As I finished reading the book to them, I realized I wanted them to go further. I wanted history to become real for them. I wanted them to realize that the Great Depression had affected their own families. These events had made a difference in the lives of their parents and grandparents. In fact, many of my students had habits and values that could be traced to the times in which these parents and grandparents had lived. I also knew that students would be able to understand the similarity between the plight of the farms in the 1930s and the problems that farmers were experiencing in northern Maine during the 1980s. With this in mind, I asked each of the students to interview a family member or acquaintance who had lived during the Depression. The initial response to the assignment was less than enthusiastic. I began to fear that I was quickly losing any ground I had gained. Fortunately, I knew enough to ask them what the problem was with the assignment.

"I don't know anyone that old."

"How am I supposed to know how to do an interview?"

"Nobody is going to want to talk to me about that. If they do, they'll be so old they won't remember what happened."

I realized the students were intimidated by the assignment. They were all used to fill-in-the-blank exercises, but they were not familiar with having to talk, listen, and learn from the experience of others—at least, not as a school assignment. I assured them that once they got people talking, they would be fine. I also reminded them that they now knew a lot about the Depression so it would be easy to build on whatever their informants told them. (I just hoped I was right!) We spent the next day brainstorming some sample interview questions that they could use to get started. The following "starter questions," written by the students, became the safety net that gave them confidence to begin their interviews:

1. What was it like for you living during the Depression?
2. What did people do for entertainment during that time?

3. How did your farming and farm equipment differ from those you use today?
4. What kind of public services were available?
5. What kind of work were you or your family doing?
6. Did you have enough food? What foods did you eat then that you don't eat now?
7. What kind of clothing did you wear? Were there articles of clothing you had to do without?
8. What were the living conditions like?
9. Did you have enough money? What were typical wages then?
10. Was it hard to get a doctor or medical care?
11. Did a lot of stores go out of business?
12. How did the Depression affect your family life?
13. What were the prices like for movies and candy?
14. Did lots of people have to quit school to try and make a living?
15. What forms of transportation were used?
16. What good things can you remember about this period of time?
17. Was school mandatory?
18. Was there much crime?
19. Did you see any difference when Roosevelt became president?
20. Do you see any comparisons between then and now?
21. What books/magazines were you reading?
22. Was there an increase in death/suicide because of the Depression?
23. Were you aware of the gangsters that came into power?
24. What appliances or utensils did you use then that you no longer use?
25. Were the Canadians affected by the Depression?
26. Could you afford to keep animals?
27. How did working conditions change during the Depression?
28. When did things start looking better?
29. What effect did the bank closings have?

As I listened to and recorded the questions the students generated, I was amazed at how much history they had absorbed about this time period. Although some of their questions might not be "typical" research questions, I knew they would certainly elicit some rich responses from the people they were interviewing. I believed that the information they gathered from this research would be even more memorable than their previous fact-finding research. After a day of practicing with tape recorders as we interviewed each other in class, the students were ready to take their book knowledge outside the classroom walls. The resulting interviews generated enthusiasm and personal connections that even I could not have predicted. The following responses are typical:

> My grandmother was so proud that I interviewed her. It had been months since I really talked to her and I had forgotten how much fun it was to listen to her. I told you I'd come and work at night to get the book printed because I can't wait to take the booklet, with my interview in it, to my grandmother. (Candy)

> I found out that the Great Depression was worse than what we have, but here are similarities: high unemployment, farmers in trouble, banks with high interest, no one has money to spare, high prices, businesses failing and an overall gloomy economy. (Kevin)

Students came back with offers from relatives who volunteered to show us how soap was made and what clothes they wore. We had folks who wanted to share their quilting and their Depression glass. In addition, the students' enthusiasm and interest was picked up by other teachers at our school. The art teacher spent two days demonstrating and allowing students to experience "hobo art." The home economics teacher presented Depression-era fashions, which resulted in a fashion show. The nutrition teacher demonstrated the cooking of "poor man's soup," and everyone sampled the food that had been a staple for many families. A former history teacher shared his collection of silent movies, and the librarian found tapes of the radio series *The Lone Ranger* and *The Shadow*. The vocational teachers demonstrated the making of hand-tooled leather signs and the rebuilding of a 1930s radio. Each day was a new experience for us as the students brought in ideas that their relatives, friends, and teachers had suggested.

The World Is Our Classroom

We were nearing the end of our unit. A student asked me if we were going to have a test on the book or if they were going to get any grades. I looked around the room, which by then looked more like a museum than a classroom, and wondered how I could grade something so far removed from the work of a traditional English class. When I shared this dilemma with my students, they suggested we have a Depression exhibit and that each of them could be graded on individual and group participation. This resulted in still more activity, and more displays. Some were typical, fairly academic projects: crossword puzzles with new words students had learned; a game with questions about *No Promises in the Wind;* a historical time line with events highlighted; a group newspaper with articles related to history, sports, entertainment and advertising with 1930s prices. There were also more creative responses. Art projects included a slide show with music—the song "Buddy, Can You Spare a Dime"; a mural with scenes from the book; and a map of the United States tracing Josh and Joey's travels. We had guest demonstrations that had resulted from the students' interviews: we made homemade soap, handled many different kinds of Depression glass, and watched as one boy's grandmother shared the art of quilt making. Everywhere there were artifacts. The room was filled with donated animal traps, quilts, clothing, dishes, wooden utensils, and farm implements. The students had discovered that the game of Monopoly had been invented during the Depression, and their handmade replicas became the game boards for our after-school Monopoly championships. Everyone's contributions were valued and celebrated because they added to our collective knowledge of this time period and of our friends and relatives who had lived through the period. I'll never forget the look on Kelly's face when her poem was chosen to adorn the cover of our history reference book—a book so much richer now that it was filled not only with historical facts, but also with the art, the interviews, and the writing done by students during these weeks.

SEARCHING FOR FOOD

Looking at the endless blue sky
  and walking down the endless road
Staring across the endless field,
  always in search of food.

Feet get tired, they ache and burn
  never wanting to go on
But they do
  always in search of food.

The nights are cold, dark and lonely,
  and the stars are no comfort,
Taking a deep breath with closed eyes trying to rest
  But, always in search of food.

No money, no house, no heat
  But, you're always in search of food.

Reflections

Long after we had gone on to read other novels, the students' work remained on the classroom walls. The copies of the historical reference book they had produced were read and reread before going to their individual homes. How much history did they learn? I think they learned more than any of us could have anticipated. They learned about the Depression; the people and places became a part of them. They learned that history could have personal meaning for them. They learned that there are lots of ways to find answers to their questions. They learned that they were valuable parts of their school and home communities. I think that the main thing they learned could be summed up with a question one of the students asked: "If this is history, why isn't it boring?" I know that during this unit, my twenty-seven general juniors became a community and they also became part of a larger community. Perhaps that is what history is really all about. How can that ever be boring?

HEATHER BLAIR

Voice for Indigenous Youth: Literature for Adolescents

Much of past and present schooling has been based on a transmission, or "banking," model of education, where the teacher has the knowledge and it is his or her job to impart it to the students. Paulo Freire (1972) criticizes this model of exclusive teacher control over classroom interaction and proposes instead "reciprocal interaction," where teachers and students share control. Implicit in Freire's model is the idea that teachers and students hold knowledge collectively and, through interaction in oral and written modes, further knowledge is negotiated (Cummins 1993). There is, in this model, a sharing of knowledge, decision making, power, and voice.

Voice in Education

What does voice mean for indigenous people in Canada and the United States? Do they have a voice in our societies or our schools? What do we as social studies teachers do to ensure that their voices are present in our classrooms?

If voice is knowledge, we need to ask ourselves what indigenous children in our classrooms know from their homes, communities, and life experiences. We also need to ask how they have learned what they know. We then need to think about how we incorporate these insights into our classrooms. In the past, indigenous children have seldom been told that what they have experienced and what they know are important and, as a result, they themselves often do not consider these things to be important. Like other minority children, they have not seen their lives mirrored in the classroom (Sims 1982). They don't hear their music in the school, see their art in the hallway, or find their leaders and heroes in the curriculum. How can anyone have voice until he or she first values what he or she knows? Indigenous people have traditionally been silenced by society through schools, and as teachers we need to find ways to help students find their voice. How can we do that?

If voice is ethics, we need to ask ourselves what ethics and processes of ethical decision making we favor in our classrooms. Nel Noddings (1988) points out that "minorities have found their voices and are beginning to suggest alternatives among moral priorities" (p. 218). What values and processes for valuing do indigenous children bring to school? How do we encourage multiple perspectives of valuing in our classrooms? How can we provide adolescents with opportunities to explore ethical issues and consider their perspectives on moral issues?

If voice is power, we need to think about what is empowering in our classrooms. Freire (1972) proposes that education for liberation starts with the learner. If education is to have any value and effect it must start with real issues for the learner. In his work with literacy programs in South America he advocates that learning can be liberating if it starts with the learner and takes a political perspective. What does this mean for our classrooms? How do we bring the real issues in the lives of indigenous students into our classrooms?

The relegation of culture to nonessential parts of curriculum is another concern. It has been suggested that children of color drop out of school because school is not related to their lives. Cohen (1993) discusses the importance of identity, differences, and racism as subjects of discussion with children of color and says teachers need to learn to facilitate student inquiry on these topics. We need to find contexts in which to explore these issues collaboratively, within and across various subject areas. We need to reexamine not only the process of teaching and learning but the content as well.

Indigenous Voice in Our Classrooms

I believe that an inquiry-based social studies program focusing on the personal and social issues in indigenous people's lives is the way to address some of these questions. An inquiry-based approach can provide a way to validate what our students know and give them the opportunity to recognize and reify their voice as experience, ethics, and power.

Creating curriculum through an inquiry approach is both challenging and exciting. Short and Burke (1991) would say that it is the foundation to real learning: "if a curriculum is truly learning centered then that curriculum is based on inquiry and the search for questions that matter to us, whether we are adults or children" (p. 55).

As an initial step towards an inquiry-based classroom you need to ask yourself the following questions: What matters to these kids? What is going on in their lives? What is bothering them? What turns them on? Your job as an inquiry-based teacher is that of an ethnographer; you try to get inside your students' heads.

One way to begin is by sharing a thought-provoking piece of literature that raises issues from your students' worlds. Subsequently, you talk about this piece; have them reflect on it; allow them to write about it; provide them with time to read a related piece that they have selected: have them read, with someone else, either the same book or related books; think; talk to each other; ask questions; and read some more. You engage them in dialogue, encourage them to talk to each other, and encourage them to search out people and experiences that will give them further insight and understanding. They might, for example, talk to an elder, visit a tribal council meeting, or interview each other. Your goal is to have them conduct literature study groups around the things that are of importance to them, interest to them, or troubling them. These topics could become the core of an authoring cycle (Short and Burke 1991) and their group explorations and presentation become the classroom focus. An inquiry approach validates students and allows them to see that their experiences are worthy of study. This, in essence, is voice as knowledge in your classroom.

It is crucial that you present your students with a range of choices of good literature and talk about these as you would with any literature study, but they must be able to choose what they read. If we are serious about having our students take control over their own learning and share power in our classrooms, then their selection of books, topics, and projects is important. Without this, we are just paying lip service to voice as power.

There is a good deal of literature, both fiction and nonfiction, that I have used to reflect the experiences of indigenous youth in my classroom. Some reflect urban or rural concerns, regional differences, or varying socioeconomic realities; some are related particularly to racial tensions and other more controversial topics.

I believe that it is important that we not censor issues based on our concept of curriculum; in order to foster our students' voice, we may have to temper our own. Our job as teachers, as the resource collectors, is to find as wide a range of literature on the emerging topics as possible. Some issues that have surfaced in my work include friendship, relationships, family, self-esteem, violence, AIDS, drugs, identity, fear, and freedom.

The literature I have included reflects a number of indigenous peoples in Canada and the United States. I have selected works that are written either by indigenous people or by those who have tried to represent their perspective. I believe that this is extremely important. If the voice of indigenous people is to be present in our classrooms, then voice through authorship is a very important consideration, as it includes both voice as knowledge and voice as ethics. How the author resolves a dilemma, what is valued, the relationships among the characters and events, for example, all give us insight into voice as ethics. These are things that we cannot assume are captured by nonindigenous authors.

Personal and Social Issues as Voice

PHILOSOPHY

I believe that the philosophy of a people is foundational to their way of life and that therefore as teachers we must begin to understand the philosophical perspective of our students.

The Yaqui people of southern Arizona, for example, are generally neglected in our curriculums and classroom discussions, yet they have rich cultural traditions and a powerful historical legacy in both Mexico and the United States. Books such as *Yaqui Deer Songs Maso Bwikam: A Native American Poetry* (1987) and *WO'I Bwikam: Coyote Songs* (1990) by Larry Evers and Felipe Molina provide a wealth of literature to lead the reader to further inquiry. Molina is a highly respected Yaqui oral historian and traditional singer whose work provides Yaqui and non-Yaqui readers with glimpses of the philosophical perspectives of his people.

Earth Elder Stories is a collection of stories retold by a Saulteaux oral historian, Alexander Wolfe (1988). This book is a wonderful example of how nonfiction can represent the voice of a people. It can be used to assist children in understanding history from a Saulteaux perspective.

Grandfather Stories of the Navahos (Callaway and Wither-spoon 1974) includes a series of narratives on Navajo history and culture. The stories include "mythological narratives, historical accounts and descriptions of things meaningful in Navaho life" (p. 5). This bilingual text is a wonderful resource for Athapaskan as well as English speakers.

IDENTITY

Identity is a complex and multifaceted concept. A child from Crownpoint, New Mexico, can be thirteen, Diné, an athlete, a sister, and bilingual, all of which contribute to her identity.

As teachers we need to be continually on the lookout for current, topical resources that reflect this complexity for indigenous youth. Magazines such as *Native People: The Arts and Lifeways* include powerful articles and interviews. For example, the article on Glafiro Perez, the deer dancer from Old Pascua, Tucson, in the Winter 1993 issue, presents a contemporary and enthusiastic view of Yaqui dances and their significance from the perspective of a young deer dancer. This young man's view of his own life would be perfect for an inquiry into identity in an indigenous urban setting.

There are as well many anthologies intended for an adult audience that are useful in a middle-years classroom. In many indigenous North American societies, stories were not age specific. People of all ages heard the same legends and stories, and their interpretation was left to the individual. Older listeners bring their life experience to a story and interpret it accordingly; younger readers interpret it quite differently. *The Southwest Corner of Time: Hopi Navajo Papago Yaqui Tribal Literature* by Larry Evers (1980) is one such book. This collection of prose and poetry from the American Southwest would be useful in any inquiry with indigenous youth.

The following anthologies of short stories and excerpts from novels written by indigenous authors are perfect for the adolescent classroom. *Talking Leaves: Contemporary Native American Short Stories* edited by Craig Lesley (1991), *All My Relations: An Anthology of Contemporary Canadian Native Fiction* edited by Thomas King (1990), and *The Lightning Within: An Anthology of Contemporary American Indian Fiction* edited by Alan Velie (1991) are all fine collections that provide a glimpse into contemporary worlds as well as times past, as informed by indigenous authors.

Toronto at Dreamer's Rock, a play written by indigenous playwright Drew Hayden Taylor (1990), brings the past, the present, and the future together through three Ojibway teenage boys. Each from a different century, they compare notes on the world around them and what it means to be Ojibway. *White Mist* by Barbara Smucker (1985) follows a similar past, present, and future theme when two Potawatomi teenagers are led to the discovery of their own history. When they return to the present they bring an increased awareness of their role as indigenous people in environmental protection.

An autobiographical account, *Halfbreed* by Maria Campbell (1973), presents the struggle of a young Metis woman coming to terms with who she was as an indigenous woman in a world that seemed to value neither. Her struggles with alcohol and drugs are very real as are her personal and political struggles. In a fictionalized autobiography, *In Search of April Raintree*, Beatrice Culleton (1983), tells of two young Metis girls who have been removed by the Child Welfare Agency from an alcoholic home and placed in foster homes. The book is a moving account of these two sisters' struggle to survive in an environment that degrades and denigrates them as indigenous people and as young women.

Something to Live For, Something to Reach For: Students of a Native Survival School by Beckie James (1989) presents the voice of indigenous teenagers. This photodocumentary features mini-autobiographies and vignettes of the lives of youth in an indigenous high school in Saskatoon, Saskatchewan. The youths tell what it means to be an indigenous person in today's world. The photographs poignantly depict who these youths see themselves to be.

Kinaaldá: A Navajo Girl Grows Up is a photodocumentary by Monty Roessel (1993) that provides an insider's view of the contemporary lives of indigenous people. In this case, the subject is a young Navajo woman's coming-of-age ceremony.

Julie of the Wolves by Jean Craighead George (1972) is a classic novel for young readers. Miyax runs away from her home in a village in northern Alaska intending to go to San Francisco. As she struggles to stay alive in the Arctic wilderness, she rethinks who she is as an Inuit person. This story, full of vigor and intensity, conveys a number of vivid images and emotions.

Jordan Wheeler's book *Brothers in Arms* (1989) includes an especially thought-provoking story, "Exposure," in which two brothers come home to the reservation to face the imminent death of the younger, who has contracted AIDS. This moving story posits many ethical and moral questions for the reader. It also deals frankly with the emotions and fears surrounding death.

The loss of traditional ways and identity figure in the book *Winners* by Mary Ellen Lang Coolura (1984). A young boy returns home to his grandfather's care on the reservation in southern Alberta after living in numerous foster homes. This story has a similar plot to *Bearstone* by Will Hobbs (1989), which is set in the mountains of Colorado. The experiences of these two boys is an interesting comparison for readers.

Honour the Sun (Slipperjack 1987) presents the fictional diary of a young Ojibway girl. The warm and pleasant events of her childhood in northern Ontario are followed by dramatic changes in her family and the turbulence of adolescence. Eventually, she goes away to school, and each visit home brings her a new perspective. In *Laughing Boy*, a classic by Oliver La Farge (1929), the author provides readers with the dilemmas in the lives of this young Navajo couple who go against the wishes of their families and confront the realities of living in the outside world.

Racism

I have found that it is helpful to begin a consideration of racism by first approaching the topic broadly; that is not to suggest we skirt the issues, but that it is helpful to look at others' lives and then examine our own. There are many good books to use to open this inquiry. Jeanette Armstrong's *Slash* (1985) is the story of Tommy, a young man growing up in a small village of indigenous people in British Columbia. Life seems idyllic until the village school closes and the children are sent to an integrated school in a nearby town. Tommy's life choices lead him to some difficult times and serious consequences, but he comes to understand the political nature of his world and who he is as an indigenous person. Don Sawyer's *Where the Divers Meet* (1988) tells how Nancy Antoine, a Shuswap Indian high school senior determined to leave the bleakness and chaos of her small town in British Columbia, spends six weeks with an elder in her community and starts to see the world from a different perspective. She gains hope in her people and in herself.

FREEDOM

Freedom is very important to young adults. For them, freedom to do things is having a sense of being able to choose for themselves and do things they want to do. Another kind of freedom that youths are cognizant of is freedom *from*. They know about freedom from harassment, freedom from responsibilities, freedom from other people's rules, and freedom from fear. Giving youth a chance to experience these kinds of things vicariously is a way to provide a valuable learning opportunity.

Journey of the Sparrows, a contemporary story written by Arizonan author Fran Leeper Buss (1991), is a moving account of young people fleeing for their lives. These young children make their way through horrendous circumstances out of Central America and Mexico to an unknown life as illegal immigrants in America. A middle school teacher in southern Arizona related that when she read this story in her class, one boy broke into tears. She later found out that someone had been taken as an illegal from his household. This underground railroad or network of people assisting others exists today as it has in the past. Barbara Smuckers' *Underground to Canada* (1977) places this kind of flight and the situation of oppressed people in a historical context of slavery. These stories used in combination with nonfictional accounts such as *The Autobiography of a Yaqui Poet* by Refusio Savala (1980), which gives the history of the Yaqui in southern Arizona, can make an interesting fiction/nonfiction text set combination for an inquiry.

Freedom sometimes comes at a very high cost, as shown in the two poignant stories of young boys running from tragedy in their own lives. In *Silent Words* by Ruby Slipperjack (1992) and *Dreamspeaker* by Cam Hubert (1978), both boys run from captivity and violence, but find that running from their fears is not the answer. Both find accepting, loving people on their journey for self-knowledge.

FRIENDSHIP

There are many stories that address cross-cultural friendship, but few that address friendship for indigenous children in indigenous communities. One such story is *A Woman of Her Tribe* by Margaret Robinson (1990). In this story, the protagonist, a young woman, leaves her isolated tribal village for the city to finish high school. She leaves behind her friends and her community roots, but on her visits home she reconnects with them and reflects both on what they mean to her as a Nootka and on the meaning of change. This book has a very positive yet realistic tone.

The *Rez Sisters* by playwright Tomson Highway (1988) presents the power of friendship among seven women from Wasaychigan Hill Reservation on Manitoulin Island, Ontario. In this play, the women discuss their lives on the "Rez" and let their dreams take them on a trip to Toronto to the "Biggest Bingo in the World."

This is just a glimpse at literature I have found helpful to address voice for indigenous youth. Of course this is by no means a review of all such literature written in North America, but they are valuable pieces to begin such an inquiry. I think we need to continue to ask ourselves as social studies teachers: If voice is knowledge, if voice is ethics, and if voice is power, what do we do in our classrooms to include voice for indigenous children?

It is important to think about how we use literature in our classrooms and how we include personal and social issues. We need to find ways to help our students face these issues head on; we need to make sure that our classrooms become a place where meaning is constructed out of our students realities. Freire suggests that a pedagogy that is participatory, critical, values oriented, multicultural, student centered, research minded, and interdisciplinary is essential for the emergence of voice (Shor 1987).

LESLIE KAHN,
PAUL FISHER,
AND DANA PITT

Teacher, Artist, Lawyer, Kids: Cycles of Collaboration and the Holocaust

IN THIS CHAPTER WE TELL A STORY—THE STORY OF OUR exploration of the Holocaust. There are three parts to our story. First we introduce you to us, our plans for the Holocaust study, and what we actually did. Next, because we believe that the development of the study is as important as the study itself, we show how we built the unit through constant meetings and private musings, how creating the unit affected our ideas about the Holocaust and education, and how the unit affected the students and they, it. We show you this through a series of journal entries we have recreated from the journals and notes we recorded during the course of the study. And we conclude by examining the key role that collaboration played in both the building and the results of the unit.

Introduction

Leslie Kahn has been an elementary school teacher in Tucson, Arizona, for fifteen years. Paul Fisher, Director of Arts Education for the Tucson/Pima Arts Council, is a performing artist and poet. Dana Pitt is a lawyer and a student in the masters program at the University of Arizona College of Education in the Department of Language, Reading, and Culture. Leslie asked Paul to join her in planning and implementing the Holocaust study for the spring semester, because she knew that Paul's involvement would allow the class to use drama effectively. She also invited Dana to become a part of the unit, because of Dana's interest in children's literature.

Leslie's sixth-grade class was, literally, a challenging group: the students were masters at questioning authority and refusing to become involved in what was going on in the classroom. They did not enjoy reading, although by the beginning of the second semester they loved writing stories. The class was composed primarily of Hispanic American students, with some Anglo, African American, and Native American children as well.

The Holocaust study was planned as a unit that would intertwine four related social studies topics and concepts: discrimination, law, civic responsibility, and culture. We envisioned the Holocaust study as a three-pronged unit interlacing literature circles (the students would select a book about the Holocaust, read it, and meet in a small group to discuss the work and plan a presentation sharing their ideas about the book with the class); drama or role-playing events with Paul; and individual or small-group inquiry projects, in which the kids would research and prepare a final presentation on a Holocaust-related topic of their choice.

We expected to ease into the study through the use of a class read-aloud that would not overtly deal with the Holocaust, but would put the class in the right frame of mind to begin the unit. As the class read the book, there would be discussion. Once they had finished, Leslie would place the kids in groups to explore one issue in greater depth and prepare a presentation on that issue for their classmates.

Paul would use acting techniques to elicit discussion and exploration of topics as they surfaced. Characterization and role-playing methods would be used to explore personality types and then to relate them to the books that were being researched and read. Improvisation would be used to create conversations about the issues "in character" (students would select characters from the literature or from history and talk through them). Scene building and performance methods would be used to make statements and comment on what had been learned.

Dana would be with the class four mornings a week. Her role would be that of observer and participant, with a primary focus on the use of literature throughout the study.

In our early planning sessions we established three goals:

1. We wanted the kids to absorb the basic facts about the Holocaust and World War II.
2. We wanted the children to become aware of themselves as members of a community (local, national, global) in which they have both responsibility and a voice.
3. We wanted to ease racial tensions in the classroom and give the kids a chance to explore issues of racial and ethnic prejudice in a nonthreatening, nonconfrontational, creative atmosphere.

In addition to meeting regularly, the three of us read extensively about the Holocaust, including both fiction and nonfiction. This exposure through literature was a major catalyst in our thinking.

Our original plans for the study served us well as a guide, but we did alter them as the unit progressed. The journal entries that follow will chronicle the changes we made and the events leading up to those changes.

Our Journal

January 31: Leslie

The kids have rifled through but not engaged with the Holocaust books I've circulated in the class. Several of the books that Paul, Dana, and I feel would make the greatest impression on the students—*The Devil's Arithmetic* (Yolen 1988), *Friedrich* (Richter 1970), and *Anne Frank: the diary of a young girl* (Frank 1952)—are too difficult for most of them to read on their own.

Sets of books are being passed around the room to ensure that everyone will have a chance to look through them. I told the kids that they must each pick a book to read in order to participate in a literature circle.

Last year the books pulled the kids into the study. Perhaps this year I need a different catalyst because the class isn't into this. For instance, when I was explaining to the kids that they needed to choose a book to read, Greg asked why we're studying war in the first place. My response was that in the sixth grade we study the world, and that looking at war is one way of understanding the world. The answer did not satisfy him. Greg chose a book, but only because he felt that he had to do so.

As I was justifying our study to Greg, I began to see his point: war does seem foreign and unimportant to him because it is not within his range of life experiences.

There is hope, however. The class is completely caught up in our read-aloud selection, *Journey of the Sparrows* (Buss 1991), which tells the story of a family of political refugees from El Salvador—their struggle to reach the United States and to survive here as undocumented aliens. Through this read-aloud experience we have begun exploring some issues central to the Holocaust (separation of family, death, difficult living conditions, political oppression, having to flee one's homeland). I hope our discussions will pave the way for the Holocaust study.

FEBRUARY 4: DANA

The kids have just begun reading their Holocaust books. They are reading *The Cay* (Taylor 1969), *The Upstairs Room* (Reiss 1972), *Summer of My German Soldier* (Greene 1973), *Snow Treasure* (McSwigan 1942), and *Sadako and the Thousand Paper Cranes* (Coerr 1977). This morning, for the first time, the students discussed the Holocaust as a group. Leslie organized the dialogue by having the children prepare questions to share with the class. (The students used their social studies textbook, which provided five pages on the topic, as a resource in developing their questions.) Leslie listed the questions on a large piece of butcher paper under the headings Who, What, Where, When, Why. A few good questions were raised, but the thing that really struck me was how little the kids knew: they brought up Napoleon and the Civil War, thinking that these topics related to the Holocaust.

In the afternoon a guest speaker from the Jewish Federation gave an overview of the Holocaust to the class. Although the speaker tried hard to engage the kids, many students appeared bored.

Paul attended the talk, and after class he met with Leslie and me to discuss the study. Our major concern is the obvious lack of enthusiasm. Paul commented that the kids need a good dose of terror. The class did show a bit of interest in some aspects of the presentation—how Hitler killed himself, the difficult living conditions in the Warsaw ghetto, and how the gas showers worked. At least it's a start.

FEBRUARY 5: DANA

Well, we thought the kids weren't listening, but they were. Leslie put up a big piece of butcher paper to record all the things the class could remember from yesterday's presentation, and the kids recalled everything the speaker told them.

The session moved from recounting to discussing as Leslie questioned the students. She particularly challenged kids who attempted to disengage from the conversation with "I don't care" comments. For instance, while talking about the "no Jews allowed" rule in the 1936 Olympics, Leslie asked the kids what they thought about this. Derrick replied, "I wouldn't care." Leslie didn't let the moment pass, but instead personalized the event for Derrick (a Hispanic American child), creating a scenario in which he had trained and qualified to be an Olympic competitor, but was denied the chance to compete because he was Hispanic. Derrick grudgingly confessed that if this happened, "I'd be mad."

FEBRUARY 10: DANA

On Tuesday a second speaker, a Holocaust survivor, talked to the class. The kids again appeared restless and bored. After school, Leslie and I met with Paul, who had again come to hear the presentation. We were still very concerned about the low interest level of the class. Paul is toying with a number of ideas about role-playing with the kids, including instances in which the laws or rules change or are unfair, as they were for Jews and other minorities under Hitler's regime. In addition, Paul would like the kids to understand how Hitler used his oratorical skills to gain power.

We decided that the children don't really have a good enough grasp of the basic facts about World War II and the Holocaust to begin in-depth role playing at this time.

FEBRUARY 10: PAUL

After talking with Leslie and Dana this afternoon, I realized that getting information to the kids is imperative to the success of my work with the class. I don't want the children to simply *act* like Holocaust characters, but rather I hope that they will *be* the characters, that they will identify with them. Such identification cannot exist unless the students bring knowledge to their role playing. For instance, children can superficially say the words "I'm hungry" and hunch over for effect, but when they have identified with starving children through inquiry the posture and the words become expressed from real knowledge.

FEBRUARY 11: DANA

Once again, we were pleased to learn that the kids had picked up almost everything the speaker said. But this time Leslie did not have to prod them for thoughts and questions; these were now freely and sometimes forcefully offered.

The first class comment was actually a very interesting complaint. The class felt that the speaker was in some sense not a qualified Holocaust survivor because she had not spent time in hiding or in a concentration camp or ghetto. She had been sent to Sweden from her home in Austria by her parents (who did die in a camp). Darcy said, "She wasn't there for it all. She just told what she heard. She didn't go through that much."

The students' rather gruesome lust for "the real thing" highlights the value of primary sources in teaching history. Leslie is concerned about this issue as it relates to the Holocaust. As she put it, "What happens when all the survivors are dead?" How are we going to preserve or recreate the immediacy of their firsthand, oral accounts?

The kids' wish for a more authentic speaker also points out a change in the atmosphere of the classroom. The students are now truly curious about the Holocaust. They want more information. During the discussion, there was a request for books "with dates and stuff about the war," and a demand for books on Nazis.

The questions were also starting to flow, ranging from factual ("What did Nazis look like?" "Are there Nazis today?") to moral ("How could the Nazis become so strong?" "Why would anyone want to be a Nazi?" "Why would people want to kill other people?") to political ("Why did America get involved so late?").

The kids even began trying out answers to their queries. For instance, Simon suggested that people might have been willing to become Nazis in order to get power and guns and "because there was nothing else to do." And Greg explained to Audrey that the Nazis killed Jewish children "so they didn't pass down their genes to the next generation."

Jewish children were a major concern during our discussion. The kids focused intently on how the Nazis treated the children and how the children survived in the camps. The students are finally beginning to personalize the study.

FEBRUARY 11: LESLIE

Paul is coming tomorrow to work with the class for the first time. I am concerned that the children's difficult relations among themselves will hamper his program. The kids are more comfortable with one another than they were in September. But group work (like role playing) can be particularly tough because often the students refuse to function cooperatively and are unable to arrive at mutual decisions.

FEBRUARY 12: LESLIE

Today Paul met with the students for the first time. It's still new to me to have him in my classroom, but we have done a lot of planning and he's very natural with the kids, so I'm fairly comfortable letting him run things.

The session went very well. Paul focused on stereotyping and racial and ethnic tensions in an extremely effective manner; he had the kids relate these issues to what they know best—themselves. He shared a story about himself in which he had been stopped by a policeman simply because he had long hair, and the students in turn offered incidents in which they or family friends had been singled out by the authorities because of their appearance. This sharing felt safe because the class was not simply repeating racial slurs, but rather was exploring how all types of stereotypes develop and how they affect our treatment of other people.

Paul found an ingenious way to introduce the children to genocide on a personal level: he had them play an ethnic cleansing game. He first reviewed with the class the Nazis' beliefs about race; then he had one child play the Nazi while the rest of the students told that child about their ethnic and racial backgrounds. The "Nazi" next compared each student's background with the official Nazi racial criteria and determined which children should be sent to a concentration camp. About 90 percent of the class was sent to a camp.

FEBRUARY 12: PAUL

When I met with Leslie's class this afternoon, I originally intended to move from our discussion of stereotyping and current events to some basic two-person role playing. But as I talked with the kids, I realized that they were not ready to dramatize the events of the Holocaust in that manner, because they had not yet thoroughly compared the troubles of those persecuted by the Nazis with the troubles in their own lives. So I improvised and came up with the ethnic cleansing game.

When I'm in a classroom, I have to be prepared to revise my plans on the spot to fit the needs of the moment.

FEBRUARY 14: LESLIE

The kids are now engaged in the Holocaust study. This is good. But have I forced the students to look at the Holocaust? Probably. Is this bad? I don't know. Am I silencing their voice when I decide that we should explore an event that many of the children have never heard of, even though the issues surrounding the event do influence their lives? Or is it enough that once I pick the general course of study, I let the kids develop their own fields of interest within the broader topic? How can I steer the kids toward a subject like the Holocaust instead of feeling like I'm dragging them toward it?

FEBRUARY 17: DANA

Yesterday Leslie mentioned that she is worried about how parents will view the Holocaust study. Her comment caught me totally off guard, as I had not and still do not see how the unit could be controversial. I told Leslie that from my vantage point as a nonteacher, teachers often seem overly concerned about how the public perceives their work, although I realize that this concern has its roots in reality.

Leslie and I discussed her thoughts further, and we determined that although the Holocaust is a major event in Jewish history, it is also a major event in world history, and the broader themes of community involvement and racial/ethnic tension should be of equal value to all groups. So we will continue as we had planned because we believe the project is a good one.

FEBRUARY 19: LESLIE

I finished reading *Journey of the Sparrows* to the class. We have had two big discussion sessions in which the kids offered all their comments about the book. I organized these comments into categories, and the students chose which categories they wished to explore further. All the kids picked the categories relating to the risks that the characters took to gain freedom and to help others.

In addition, two of the Holocaust book groups, the ones reading *The Cay* and *Sadako*, have begun meeting to talk about the works; the other groups are still in the reading phase.

FEBRUARY 19: PAUL

After school today, Dana, Leslie, and I met at a bookstore to purchase a signed copy of *Rescuers: Portraits of Moral Courage in the Holocaust* (Block and Drucker 1992), a book recounting the stories of individuals who helped Jews in Nazi-dominated Europe during Hitler's reign. While thumbing through the book in the store, I was struck by the authors' use of four terms to categorize the participants in the Holocaust: murderers, victims, rescuers, and bystanders. I realized that most Germans and members of other Nazi-occupied countries in Europe had been bystanders, and I thought we could perhaps explore with the kids what it means to be a bystander. Why do people remain bystanders instead of taking action? What kinds of risks are involved in breaking out of the bystander character?

FEBRUARY 19: DANA

Paul's idea about bystanders and taking risks ties in perfectly with the kids' interest in risks and choices in *Journey of the Sparrows*. The students are captivated by the notion of risking one's own security to help another, but they don't all think that the risk is worth taking. For instance, Greg noted that he would not have gone out of his way to help the undocumented family in *Journey*.

MARCH 1: LESLIE

The kids really enjoyed their sessions with Paul last week. He had them act out emotions, as well as physical states like cold and tired, as a precursor to role-playing Holocaust-related characters. One problem is that the students are inexperienced with drama. So, before Paul's next visit, although I don't know a lot about drama, I am going to work with the class on things like speaking clearly, staying in character, and not giggling (the biggest problem).

I really feel like Paul and I are teaching well together now. I'm more comfortable interrupting when I think we're headed the wrong way, and I think that Paul welcomes my input.

March 2: Dana

An interesting exchange took place today. It seems that some of the kids have been breaking the rules at lunch by playing tackle rather than flag football. When Leslie asked the children about this, she was told that Derrick convinced them to play tackle. Leslie, without mentioning the Holocaust, noted that it's amazing how one person's voice can sway others to follow him in something they know they shouldn't do. At this point, James interjected, "It's like Hitler. . . . It's like you kind of want to do it, but know you shouldn't, and then someone pushes you to do it."

March 5: Leslie

All the Holocaust book groups have finished reading and discussing their books, and they are now preparing presentations, as are the *Journey of the Sparrows* groups. I am glad the kids can move between groups so easily.

I used to view presentations as simple sharing sessions in which the kids tell their classmates what they've learned. Recently, however, I have come to place a greater value on them. My change in thinking is twofold. First, I believe that presenting allows the kids to utilize many sign systems—math, music, art, drama, and language (Harste and Short with Burke 1988). I think that the use of multiple sign systems provides the students with options to explore the topics we're studying through a variety of channels. And this enlarged scope broadens the children's ability to expand their thinking about the concepts they're examining.

Second, I have determined that presenting is not just an end but also a means of making continued connections, connections with the material and with those observing the presentation. The presentation is not an explanation of an idea or concept, but rather an exploration. This exploration is begun by the presenter and built on through the responses of the observers. I now view presentations as part of a learning cycle, rather than summations of learning.

Paul has also affected the way that I (and the students) see presentations. His emphasis on dramatic skills and creating a coherent dramatic character and story format has caused us to focus on the act of presenting as well as the content of the presentation. In fact, the kids are beginning to accept the idea that just like the stories they write, presentations can be shown to the class, critiqued, and then reworked and shared again. For instance, the *Sadako* group put on the play it had created, and Paul stopped the group a number of times to offer suggestions. James, one of the group members, said, "We messed up, but I think Mr. Fisher made it [their play] better."

MARCH 9: PAUL

Leslie recently shared her interest in sign systems with me. I believe that this concept ties into my thinking about art and the artist as learning tools in the classroom. It seems to me that within the classroom, art can function as a tool to foster creativity, as well as being the end product of creativity.

I view art and the artist (someone like myself who shares artistic expertise with a class) as catalysts. Artistic endeavors, like our role playing and dramatic presentations, promote change in the classroom through two routes. First, they provide the students with reasons to inquire about issues and facts related to the art. For instance, in preparation for the *Sadako* presentation, some members of the group went to the library and researched the atomic bomb because they needed to know more about it in order to create their drama. And second, such artistic adventures engage the children emotionally and provide them with a safe medium through which they can express and explore their feelings about the subject being studied. In Leslie's class the kids can try out being a Nazi or a concentration camp prisoner through role playing.

Thus, I think that my job as the artist in Leslie's classroom is not necessarily to make the kids better actors, but rather to facilitate the transference of their knowledge about the Holocaust into another medium, which, I hope, will further engage them and cause them to pursue their inquiries. However, I do want to bring to Leslie and her students the basic artistic skills and concepts necessary for them to continue using art as an effective learning tool after I am gone.

Artists pursue questions as doggedly as they follow visions. Studios are designed to encourage and support risk taking. I believe that a classroom should be run as an artist's studio. An artist's studio is set up to facilitate creativity and discovery. Since inquiry, creativity, and risk taking are key components of learning, the relationship between classroom and studio seems natural to me.

Moreover, a studio is an environment conducive to maximizing resources. The classroom should be similarly structured to offer students the many diverse resources needed for learning. Thus, just as artists gather resources to make art in their studios, students should be able to pull together classroom resources—books, the teacher, other students, and so forth—to create and pursue learning.

MARCH 10: DANA

The kids now have some definite ideas about the Holocaust: the Jews were victims, the Nazi soldiers were killers, the German civilians liked what the soldiers did but didn't want to do it themselves, Hitler convinced his followers through lies that Jews were bad, and Hitler used his oratorical skills to gain and keep power.

So far the children have absorbed information, but they have only a one-dimensional perspective on the Holocaust and World War II. I am concerned that they see all Germans as evil and all Jews as victims. (Even though the kids know that the Nazis persecuted groups other than the Jews, when role playing they invariably use a Jew as a victim.)

In today's role play with Paul, in which the children paired up and conducted interviews, one student portrayed a neutral interviewer and the other a character from the Holocaust. Amanda and Mario created a chilling but typically one-sided view of a German civilian.

MARIO: What do you do?

AMANDA: I sit around the house and watch people get killed.

MARIO: You kill people?

AMANDA: No, I watch.

MARIO: Why do you watch?

AMANDA: Because I like to see what the German soldiers do to the Jews.

MARIO: Would you like to be a German soldier?

AMANDA: No.

MARIO: Why not?

AMANDA: Because they kill people.

I think it's important that the children realize that not everything was so clear-cut. There were Germans who weren't Nazis, and there were Jews who collaborated with the Nazis.

Despite their lack of a complete picture of the Holocaust, the kids seemed to make a big jump today in their dramatic skills. They now create logical dialogues, and they seldom fall out of character.

MARCH 15: LESLIE

The kids are working on comic-strip-like storyboards. The storyboards are Paul's suggestion; he thinks that we may be able to develop some of them into dramas. So we have asked each student to create a story or scene related to the issues surrounding World War II and the Holocaust. Because we want the children to feel free to break away from the 1930s–1940s European setting, we have encouraged them to include the themes we've been discussing within any framework they want.

I am going to ask the kids to write down the questions they have about the Holocaust or other related issues. I will use these questions as the basis for setting up inquiry study groups. They seem more than ready to pursue this topic in more depth.

MARCH 18: LESLIE

I have been talking with Dana about the intersection between my emphasis on multiple sign systems and Paul's theory of the classroom as artist's studio. Dana thinks that the two ideas are quite compatible. She views the classroom-studio as a place that encourages the use of all sign systems because the goal of both classroom and studio is to promote broader inquiry and the discovery of more complete, complex answers by students.

I then mentioned to Dana that creativity seems to be at the core of both sign systems and the classroom as studio because it is creativity, as both product and process, that makes a rich class environment. Dana responded that I provide an environment with a variety of media to encourage and support students. She commented that generating an artist's studio means making a specific environment in which students create, not passing on to them creativity as a discrete skill.

MARCH 23: DANA

The book presentations are really coming along. The variety of media used and ideas shared has made it possible for everyone to stay interested in all the groups' offerings. I think Leslie's concept of presentations as a vehicle for continued learning is being exemplified in our classroom.

The children who read *The Upstairs Room* developed a successful presentation. The book chronicles the relationship between two Jewish girls and the Gentile family that hid them from the Nazis. As a way of focusing on the fears of the characters, Karen, Glenn, Duncan, and Lee made a list of things that in their own lives scared them. When the group first presented, their introductions and the content of their presentation were disorganized. Nevertheless, the class was very responsive to their presentation. Many students asked questions, which helped the group sort out what they were doing and why they were doing it. They reworked their presentation and put together a choral reading of the list, which they presented and explained with confidence.

The students' willingness to offer suggestions to the *Upstairs Room* group is representative of a new atmosphere in the class. The kids are beginning to work together more comfortably. When a presentation isn't going well, we hear more constructive comments from a wider array of kids than earlier in the semester.

MARCH 26: LESLIE

The students are now very involved in their inquiry projects. Several kids are learning about Hitler; this is great because the entire class finds him fascinating. Other children are studying a variety of issues, including concentration camps, the types of planes used in World War II, the atomic bomb, nutrition and starvation, art created during the Holocaust, and how children played in the ghetto and the camps. Derrick's topic is particularly pertinent and interesting. He is comparing Nazi youth groups with today's gangs.

The only problem we're having is with resources. Dana and I have been gathering books at the public and university libraries. Still, we have had a hard time finding quality materials that the students can read. So we are working with what we've got. Dana and I are helping the students negotiate the difficult materials by reading aloud and/or picking out accessible parts of the books. The children's interest level is so high that they are not intimidated by the advanced literature; they use the books as best they can without getting frustrated. For instance, Donna used as a resource a very scholarly adult book on play during the Holocaust, *Children and Play in the Holocaust: Games among the Shadows* (Eisner 1988). She focused on the pictures, songs, and poems and ignored the more difficult text.

None of the kids has begun working on the presentation of a project yet. Because of my interest in sign systems, I am already telling them they can present using any medium they like.

March 26: Dana

Paul shared with the class his conceptualization of the murderer, victim, bystander, rescuer model. He replaced murderer with criminal because the latter is a broader, more inclusive term.

Paul explained the categories to the class and had the students list Holocaust characters who fit under each one. The kids grasped the concept quite quickly. For instance, Donna used only one sentence to role-play a bystander. She exclaimed, "Thank God it wasn't me!"

We think this model may be helpful in loosening up the kids' limited view of the Holocaust (all Germans were bad, etc.). For instance, we could discuss how these terms apply to the Jews who ran and policed the ghettos, and to Germans or other Europeans who, in order to protect their families, joined the Nazi party or refused to help those persecuted by the Nazis.

April 1: Paul

Leslie and Dana shared with me their thoughts about using the criminal, victim, bystander, rescuer categories to push the children's thinking about the Holocaust to a more sophisticated level. So today I began by asking the kids why a Jew would be a guard or policeman in the ghetto. The students immediately came up with a perceptive list of reasons: to get money, to get food, to get respect, and to get power.

I then asked if the children would be friends with someone who turned against his or her people as those Jews who worked with the Nazis in the ghettos or those who turned in other Jews did. The class said no. So I then asked if the Holocaust came to

Tucson today, would it be acceptable if the students' parents turned others in to the Nazis to save their families. Mitchell responded that it would be "good and bad." Greg said, "It's a good decision. As long as you're safe, you don't care about anybody else." I asked Greg if he really believed what he just said and he replied, "Sometimes."

Our discussion then moved to the Nazis and how they could stomach committing such atrocities. Again the kids came up with thoughtful suggestions. For instance, Greg said they did it to get power. Derrick said that the soldiers did it to keep from being killed themselves, and James said of the Nazis, "They couldn't go to sleep just like that; I'm sure they had nightmares."

After our discussion, I had the kids pick one of the four categories—criminal, victim, bystander, or rescuer—and create a character to fit it by writing three or four sentences about the character's situation and state of mind. Some of the students acted out their characters.

I think the session today was very successful. The children expressed ideas that we hadn't heard before, and they now seem to be viewing the participants in the Holocaust as complex characters.

APRIL 1: DANA

Today Leslie and I pulled together a group of picture books and one short novel relating to the issues the class has been discussing in the Holocaust study. Leslie is going to use the books as a read-aloud text set that will serve as the final part of the study.

Originally, Leslie intended to have only one read-aloud book, *Journey of the Sparrows*. Since beginning the study of the Holocaust, however, she found her plans changing according to the needs and interests of her students. After reading *Journey of the Sparrows* to the class, she read *The Girl Who Loved Caterpillars* (Merrill 1992). This is a picture book about a girl in twelfth-century Japan who refused to conform to the feminine standards of the time. Leslie chose the book because the choices made by the main character parallel on a smaller scale the choices made by the individuals who refused to follow the Nazis in twentieth-century Europe.

Leslie followed this up with the picture book *The Children We Remember* (Abells 1983), which provides an overview of the lives of Jewish children during World War II; *Hiroshima No Pika* (Maruki 1980), a picture book about the dropping of the atomic bomb on Hiroshima; and *The Boys Who Saved the Children* (Baldwin 1981), the story of a group of Jewish boys in a ghetto who devise a plan to prevent the ghetto children from being sent to a concentration camp. Leslie read these three books to provide the class with more information about World War II and the Holocaust. The students discussed each book after they had finished hearing it, and shared their questions and comments, just as they would in smaller literature circles.

Since there are still many picture books that the students have looked at but not read, we decided that it would be appropriate to use some of these books as the basis for the closing of the study. We have put the books into a sequence—*Terrible Things* (Bunting 1980), *Faithful Elephants* (Tsuchiya 1988), *The Friendship* (Taylor 1987), *Rose Blanche* (Gallaz and Innocenti 1985), *An Angel for Solomon Singer* (Rylant 1992), *Let the Celebrations Begin* (Wild 1991), and *The Great Peace March* (Near 1993), which we hope will suggest to the class a positive note upon which to end the unit.

Each book will be read aloud by Leslie, after which there will be a class discussion. Then all the read-alouds will be discussed as a set, with the class pulling out important issues or themes. Finally, the kids will split into small groups to explore specific topics and prepare presentations, just as they did for *Journey*.

APRIL 15: DANA

The inquiry projects are coming along. Most of the students have finished their research and their projects appear to be taking a variety of forms—stories, diaries, drawings, reports, poems, and dioramas.

James and Melanie are building a model of what they think Hitler's home looked like. Jessica and Amanda are making a replica of a concentration camp. Both groups also have an accompanying report or diary. The four of them are now considering placing their dioramas next to each other and presenting jointly to show the contrast between Hitler's life-style and life in a concentration camp.

The two groups' awareness of what the other is doing and their willingness to combine their efforts to make a more interesting presentation are just two examples of the recent increase in positive interaction among the students; they seem to be developing a new degree of respect for one another.

APRIL 27: LESLIE

We have been having good discussions about the books I've been reading aloud. Several of the works have taken us beyond the Holocaust by placing issues we've been studying in a different context. For instance, in *The Friendship,* an Anglo shopkeeper in the Jim Crow South shoots an African American man because the African American had called him by his first name. The Anglo man is goaded into the shooting by a group of Anglo men.

Greg summed up the shopkeeper's actions by explaining, "It's like when you're fighting and you don't want to throw that punch and they encourage you and you do it anyway." Evan compared the story to the Holocaust, stating, "Before the Holocaust, the Jews were friends with all kinds of people and then those people went against them."

Today we read *An Angel for Solomon Singer,* a picture book about a lonely man living in New York City who finds companionship and his dreams in a cafe. The kids really picked up on the idea that dreams and friendship can keep an individual afloat when times are hard. They related this concept to the Holocaust by noting that dreams and hope were essential to the survival of many people in the concentration camps.

I am very pleased that we have been able to include books like these, which stretch the boundaries of our study by allowing the children to stretch their thinking about the issues we have been exploring.

APRIL 29: LESLIE

We have finished all the read-alouds. Today I recorded the kids' comments about the books, just as I did with their ideas about our first read-aloud, *Journey of the Sparrows.* Then I had the students organize the ideas into the categories they will be exploring in small groups. They had a bit of a hard time at first, but they ultimately came up with five classifications: hope/freedom, war, power, death, and Jews/children.

MAY 3: DANA

Paul met with the class in the afternoon. After Leslie suggested that he work with the read-aloud groups on dramas relating to their themes, he had each group quickly develop a location, characters, and a scene or event that tied in with their topic.

The pieces the kids put together were good. They are now adept at efficiently pulling together a complete story and portraying it competently. The most impressive drama was done by the "power group," James, Greg, Cedric, and Dale. They recreated the beating of Reginald Denny during the L.A. riots. They closed the scene with the following line spoken by one of the attackers to Denny as he stood over him after the beating: "Don't you feel better? I do."

Power has developed into a big issue for the kids during this study. They have always included it in their lists of motivating factors for the Nazis as a group, and they have been trying to pick Hitler apart to learn how he obtained so much power. I am not sure why they have this fascination with power, but it may stem from the fact that they feel shut out of the power structure they see controlling their lives. In any event, it's great to see them grapple with an issue that means so much to them.

May 7: Leslie

The inquiry groups are now presenting their projects. As with the earlier presentations, the kids are being exposed to a vast amount of information because of the variety of topics. For instance, Greg studied the art created during the Holocaust and presented his findings by displaying the art that he created after doing his research. Donna created a poster about how children played in the ghettos and camps. She read two poems aloud, one taken from a book about the games children played during the Holocaust and one she wrote about the games she plays.

The kids are really concentrating on speaking clearly and coherently. Paul's presence in the class has made a tremendous difference in both the students' surface drama skills and in their ability to use presentations as tools that create deeper understanding of the topic being presented.

Today was Paul's last visit to the class. We concluded his sessions by continuing the read-aloud dramas that we began on Monday. The dramas seemed to help the kids explore their chosen subjects. They have been practicing their pieces all week, and they produced their best dramatic work this afternoon.

MAY 14: LESLIE

The Holocaust study and the school year are coming to a close too quickly. The read-aloud groups have begun presenting and although they really need a bit more time, we have to finish before the end of school next week. Despite the rush, the students are working quite efficiently together. I think their ability to focus intently on their work is the result of the new feeling of mutual respect and trust that has developed over the course of the semester.

Conclusion

The hallmark of this experience for us has been the vast amount of explicit communication that continued throughout the planning and implementation of the study. Leslie planned the class schedule so that she and Dana had time for a twenty-minute talk on the days Dana was in the classroom. Similarly, Dana, Leslie, and Paul met whenever Paul visited the class as well as several times outside of class.

Our communication developed into a cycle of collaboration. We would meet and share our ideas, go off and ruminate on what we'd discussed, maybe do some reading or writing related to our discussion, and then meet again. In this fashion, we shaped the Holocaust study, our ideas about the Holocaust, the teaching of the Holocaust, and teaching in general.

For instance, Leslie deepened her understanding of the use of multiple sign systems by comparing this concept with Paul's notion of the classroom as artist's studio. Her review then led her to consider more carefully the place where she felt the two ideas intersect, that being creativity. Also, Leslie's thinking affected her teaching; she became more intent on inviting the students to use multiple sign systems, and she began examining new ways to encourage creativity in her classroom.

Communication and collaboration were also hallmarks of the students' experience. The Holocaust study was really several small communication/collaboration processes rolled into one big one. In each of the four major components of the study—the literature circle, the *Journey of the Sparrows* groups, the inquiry projects, and the read-aloud groups—the students would convey their ideas to their classmates through discussion and presentation. These ideas took new form as the kids received comments from us and one another, did reading or writing, and then returned to the discussion or presentation forum. In essence, the children's method of examining the Holocaust mirrored our own process.

This collaborative cycle allowed the students to actively seek answers to their questions. But perhaps more important, it generated an environment that was conducive to learning—one of trust, respect, comfort, and enthusiasm. As the students acted in concert to share their queries and theories about the Holocaust, they grew together. The classroom developed into a true community in which each member had value and a voice.

Paul refers to such a community as the ensemble. Just as artists meet and mix to build a group performance, a classroom ensemble comes together to share a learning experience in which the individual is nurtured, consensus is discovered, and success is shared.

ELIZABETH NOLL

Constructing Knowledge Through Multiple Perspectives: Sixth Graders as Investigators

STUDYING THE COUNTRIES OF THE WORLD IS STANDARD fare in most upper elementary grades. In the middle school where I taught, sixth grade social studies focused on the history, government, economy, and geography of as many countries as a class could get through in nine months. I found myself teaching social studies much the same way I had been taught and the way my colleagues taught, chapter by chapter, country by country, through the textbook. While I knew that my students were picking up a considerable amount of information, I wasn't satisfied. They knew facts about apartheid in South Africa and about the bombing of Hiroshima, for example, but for them these were just lessons in their social studies textbook.

I wanted my students to have opportunities to learn how conditions, like apartheid and war, affect real people. I wanted them to look at what they already know and raise questions about what they wanted to know. I also wanted them to make personal connections with their learning and to approach it from a number of perspectives. I was convinced that learning in these ways was important; I just wasn't sure how to provide for it in my classroom. In this chapter, I describe how I began to move away from textbook-dominated teaching and teacher-dominated learning to a more learner-centered approach, one that was more consistent with my beliefs.

Getting Started

Though I was ready for change, I decided to start slowly, so I chose one country for the whole class to study. Because my school was located in a small community originally settled by Scandinavians, I chose Sweden and began with some of my own research. I interviewed Clare, a local Swedish woman. During the interview I began to get a sense of the direction I wanted my class to take. Clare's stories about her childhood, schooling, and eventual emigration to the United States fascinated me. The more I listened to her, the more I wanted to learn. My interest in Sweden was no longer just for the sake of developing a unit. I was genuinely curious about Clare. As she and I talked, I realized how important this experience was. I began to see interviewing as a way for my students to make personal connections. I told Clare what I was thinking, and she readily agreed to be interviewed by my students. Later, with her help, I contacted other Swedish descendants in our community who were also willing to be interviewed or to speak to the entire class.

Next, I enlisted the help of librarians at my school and the local public library. Together we selected books about Sweden. I wanted the students to come to know the country from multiple perspectives, so we chose fiction and nonfiction adult books as well as picture books. I gathered folktales and contemporary stories, historical accounts and travelogues. In addition, I borrowed filmstrips and audio tapes and ordered two videos from the state film library.

To begin our study of Sweden, I told the students about my visit with Clare. I shared some of the stories she had told me. I talked with my students about the difference between learning from a primary source such as Clare and learning from a textbook. My goal was to have the students be able to compare viewpoints from multiple sources of information, the textbook being only one source.

On a large piece of butcher paper my students and I listed other possible sources of information:

Interviews
Textbooks
Nonfiction, fiction, and poetry about Sweden
Swedish music
Tourism brochures
Newspaper and magazine articles about Sweden
Guest speakers
Films and filmstrips
Television specials on Sweden
Cookbooks

The student who suggested reading cookbooks explained that in one of her family's cookbooks the recipes from other countries included information on their significance to those countries. Two students said they already knew stories about Sweden, having heard them from either a grandparent or a neighbor.

It was clear that more than a few of the students already possessed some knowledge about Sweden. This was not surprising, given where we lived. Many students were of Swedish or Norwegian ancestry, and most of them were familiar with the annual Midsummer festival held in a nearby farming community. What was surprising was the realization that I may have been ignoring the students' background knowledge of other topics up to then.

I asked the students to meet in small groups and share what they already knew about Sweden. Their desks were arranged in groups of three to five, which made it easy for them to work together. Each group had large sheets of paper, and they all were expected to jot down their ideas with a different-colored marker. The students were familiar with brainstorming. They understood that its purpose was to list as many ideas as possible, withholding judgment even if ideas seemed to conflict. There was no one recorder, no one person in charge of verifying individual involvement. At the end of the brainstorming time, it was clear from the different-colored notes that everyone had been actively involved.

After the students finished brainstorming, they presented what they knew to the class. The groups had organized their information in different ways: webs, lists, diagrams, and so forth. The students found it interesting that even within our one class there were different perspectives. For example, one group had written that living conditions in Sweden were crowded, while another referred to the space and beauty of the country. After some discussion the class agreed that both views might be accurate, based on different experiences. As with our list of possible sources, the students' brainstorming sheets were hung on the wall so they could be referred to and added to at any time.

Early the next day, Chris walked into the classroom carefully bearing a package. Inside was a family heirloom: a diary written by Chris's great-aunt about her life as a girl and young woman growing up in Dalarna, Sweden. Chris also had a separately bound English translation of the diary. At supper the evening before, Chris had told her family about our study of Sweden, and afterward her mother had retrieved the old diary and the translation from a trunk in the attic. That day we all listened as Chris read aloud from the translated diary about a young girl named Anna who dreamed of the Midsummer Festival during the long, dark winter days in Sweden. We laughed at the antics of her mischievous younger brothers and felt a certain amount of awe at the extent of her household and farming chores. The personal connections I had hoped for were starting to be made.

Before Chris took the diary home, all of the students had an opportunity to look at it. Fortunately, we were able to keep the translated copy in the classroom for the next few weeks. It proved to be a popular piece of reading. Even after we had read it aloud, individual students borrowed it to reread favorite sections.

Throughout our study students added to the original source list and brainstorming charts. Lists grew longer and webs more intricate as the students added what they were learning through reading and discussion. One day I noticed that an addition had been made to our list of prospective sources: diaries.

I set aside time daily for the groups to browse and read the library books. I also placed several audio cassette tapes, filmstrips, and a box of slides in our listening center along with the necessary equipment for individual or paired viewing. I posed questions for the students to consider as they read, viewed, and discussed:

Were there any contradictions in the information your sources provided?

How did the perspectives you found differ?

What would you like to know more about?

For about a week the students read and shared responses to books, listened to tapes, and watched films and filmstrips. We then came together to talk about the different perspectives they had discovered so far. A number of students spoke of the impersonal tone of the language used in some informational books as compared to the more personal approach of other books. One student described the different perspectives his group had found among fiction books, in particular folktales. They all enjoyed reading Swedish folktales and were surprised at the amount of information they were learning through them. Others remarked on the different perspectives contained in historical accounts. Searching for the perspective from which a text is written helped my students to become more critical readers. As they discovered what appeared to be conflicting information, they looked at the purpose of each piece in order to understand the ambiguity rather than simply assuming that one source must be wrong.

In addition to small group and class discussions, each student kept a learning log. In these logs, or journals, the students wrote about topics that interested them, reacted to readings and guest speakers, and evaluated themselves as learners. Each

week I read and responded in writing to the logs. This enabled
me to communicate regularly with each student and to keep
track of individual progress. It also assured me that things were
going well.

Exploring Special Interests

One day after nearly two weeks, I asked my students, "Based on
what you've learned about Sweden so far, are there topics you
find especially interesting and would like to learn more about?"
Many of the students responded with quite specific ideas:

> The Midsummer Festival
> Swedish handcrafts
> Traditional and contemporary Swedish children's games
> Sports in Sweden
> Schooling in Sweden
> Sweden's involvement in wars
> Farming techniques in Sweden
> When and why Swedes emigrated to the United States
> Early Swedish settlements in the United States

We discussed how they might go about exploring these and
other special interests. I believe in giving students choice in
what they learn; I also believe it is important to encourage them
to think about *how* they might learn. Students develop responsibility as learners by being allowed to decide "what to learn,
what to engage with, in what order to approach any given set of
tasks and how to go about any particular task" (Cambourne
1988, pp. 83–84). Later, as I became more comfortable with sharing the responsibility for these decisions with my students, I
broadened the scope to integrate different countries around a
common theme. This allowed the students even greater choice.
However, I was not ready for that yet. For now, focusing just on
Sweden was more easily manageable for both the students and
me. In addition, the study of Sweden was providing a basis for
future planning.

Given a choice, a few students wanted to continue reading books about Sweden that they had started earlier. Others asked to have more guest speakers visit the class. Two were interested in finding someone who could teach them Swedish dancing and crafts. A large number were anxious to begin interviewing individuals about their areas of interest. The students varied in how they wanted to carry out their inquiries. A few wanted to work by themselves, but most wanted to work in pairs or small groups. After discussing different options, the students began making plans on their own and describing them in their learning logs (see Figure 4–1).

I want to find out all about sports in sweeden and since Josh and David do too, we decied to work together. So far I've found information on sports in only two books but one of them had alot, Josh is going to bring in a National Geographic article he has. Skiing is big in Sweden especially long distance cross contry races, None of us could find anything about baseball, We want to find out if Kids play baseball there and also if there's a national sport. They have sports high schools in sweden! I really want to find out more about those. what we want to do is interview someone who has lived in sweden and played sports like in High school or college.

Figure 4–1
Excerpt from learning log

Meanwhile, I had been busy seeking out more people who would be willing to be interviewed. Planning ahead for future studies, I also kept a list of people from countries other than Sweden who were interested in meeting with my students. Our community was small, with only about ten thousand people including the university population, so initially I had no idea just how many people I would be able to find. I went to a variety of sources; I called the senior citizens center and nursing home, spoke with university personnel who were in regular contact with international students, and sent home letters explaining our study to the parents of my students. I was surprised at the number of positive responses. Many people were willing to volunteer their time to talk with the students about their native countries and cultures. Some had lived in the United States for years; others were visiting or attending school on temporary visas. In addition, there were people who were familiar with other countries through travel and could offer a traveler's perspective. A few individuals volunteered to teach traditional handcrafts, songs, and dances. I kept track of all volunteers on three-by-five cards in a small file box that was easily accessible to the students.

I also made a point of keeping the principal informed about the learning activities going on in my classroom. I explained my plans for the students' interviews, most of which would take place out in the community, and sent him a copy of my letters to parents. He was enthusiastic and supportive and became a regular visitor to our classroom.

Interviewing

Interviewing plans were taking shape. The students first met to decide on the interview questions. Then they contacted individuals and arranged an interview time. Three parents had offered to drive students to interviews. Two groups of students got permission to walk to their nearby interview sites. Others arranged their interviews for after school when I was free to drive.

Keeping track of who was to be where and when was a nightmare until I made a large laminated schedule and hung it on the wall. Individual students and groups recorded their own comings and goings. We established a few ground rules. Students who had to miss other classes were responsible for making up work. If an interview could only be scheduled during an exploratory class such as music or art, the student was required to get permission from the teacher to be absent from that class.

The students handled the responsibility well. They regarded their jobs as interviewers seriously and were punctual about their appointments. Some chose to tape-record their interviews; others took notes. Several students took pictures or slides, and one even videotaped a man who showed farming tools used by his great-grandfather in Sweden. Returning to the classroom and reviewing their findings, a number of the students came up with new questions that resulted in follow-up interviews and more reading and discussion. Generating new questions as earlier ones are answered is one sign of successful inquiry (Short and Burke 1991). Another sign for me was the charged atmosphere in our classroom. The students were excited and self-directed as they learned about things that truly interested them.

There were a few hitches. In one interview a student forgot to push the record button on her tape recorder and didn't realize it until after returning to school. Another time, a heavy rain prevented one group from going to their interview. The progress of another group was hampered by personality conflicts. Yet all of these problems and others that arose were resolved rather easily.

It was thrilling to observe my students' enthusiasm and sense of purpose. Yet, as a teacher who had been used to carefully controlling the activity in the classroom, at first it wasn't easy for me to move from the role of director to that of facilitator. As Freeman and Nofziger (1991) observe, relinquishing control can be a rather difficult, even frightening, experience for teachers who have become comfortable with and adept at determining the kinds of learning that will take place in their classrooms. There were times that I found the amount of talk and movement in the room overwhelming. Resisting the impulse to call for quiet, I learned to first take stock of what my students were actually doing. By quietly and carefully observing groups and listening to conversations, I was able to reassure myself that the activity was constructive and purposeful. If a group was "off task," I spent a few minutes helping them redirect themselves. Sometimes a simple "Tell me what you are working on now" or "What are you going to do next?" was enough to get the students back on track.

As the students became increasingly knowledgeable about their chosen topics, I encouraged them to consider how they might want to share what they had learned with the rest of the class. They discussed a variety of options. I recommended that they include the issue of perspectives. How would they describe the perspective of the person they interviewed? How had their own perspective regarding Sweden been influenced by their reading, discussions, and interviews?

A few of the students chose to write and illustrate reports on what they had learned. Others gave oral presentations. One of these presentations was a debate between two Swedish neighbors arguing the merits of emigrating to the United States at the turn of the century. The three students interested in the Midsummer Festival presented an elaborate puppet play with historical narration. Another group reenacted the interview they had conducted and described the value of the interview process. Two groups presented their findings with annotated photo and slide displays. One of these was accompanied by a taped description in which their interviewee's voice was interwoven. And one group used paints to demonstrate the techniques they had learned about traditional Swedish design.

Evaluation

Evaluation of the students and of our study of Sweden was ongoing. The students and I regularly talked about how things were going—what was working well and what should be changed. As we concluded the study, I asked them to reflect on their individual learning in their logs. What new insights did they have as a result of their reading, discussions, and interviews? Had their special interests been addressed to their satisfaction? What new questions did they now have? I also asked them to evaluate their own effort, involvement, and commitment during the course of the study (see Figure 4–2).

Besides evaluating themselves, the students were evaluated by their peers and by me. Each student or group of students received oral feedback from their classmates at the conclusion of their final presentation. I, too, responded to the students, usually in written form with a follow-up conference. For the final quarterly evaluation, I saved a copy of my comments along with samples of the students' work, including certain entries from their learning logs.

The students were enthusiastic and unanimous regarding their learning experiences. Many commented that, before

Learning about Sweeden has been one of the best things so far this year. I had so much fun and learned a lot. Doing everthing ourselfs like choosing what we want to read and who our partners will be and finding stuff on our own was so much better than before. Being able to actually talk with a Swedish person made me feel like I really understand Sweeden. Its like now I'm sort of an expert on Sweden, especially on Mid-Summer.

Figure 4–2
Excerpt from student's self-evaluation

engaging in this study, they had considered social studies boring. Now they ranked it high. Previously, my students had had few opportunities to develop their own questions and act on their own interests, to satisfy their curiosity through real investigation. I believe that being allowed to choose what and how they would learn was a major factor in redefining their attitude towards social studies.

We also talked about ideas for improvement for future studies of countries. A number of the students thought that the interviewing should be started earlier in the study. Others wondered if they could interview more than one person in order to compare perspectives on similar issues. Several students asked about having pen pals from other countries.

Many of these ideas and others were implemented in future studies. Later that year several groups wanted to share their final presentations on Sweden and other countries with additional audiences, and I was able to arrange for them to speak at an educators' conference. By responding seriously to my students' suggestions I showed them that they really did have an active role in directing their learning. For their part, my students had shown me that my beliefs about the teaching of social studies from multiple perspectives could be successfully carried out in practice.

Conclusion

The opportunities to explore different perspectives, and to raise and pursue their own questions, gave my students—and me—much broader and richer understandings than would have been possible from simply reading our textbook chapter. Through their varied reading experiences, discussions, learning logs, interviews, and final sharing, my students constructed knowledge that had personal meaning for them. This knowledge was about more than a country. It was also about themselves as capable learners.

SANDY KASER

Creating a
Learning Environment
that Invites Connections

IN THIS CHAPTER I BEGIN BY SHARING THE EXPERIENCES and questions that led me to want to support my fifth-grade students in making connections between individual cultural backgrounds and our classroom learning. I became interested in how literature could serve as a bridge for making those connections, and explored the possibilities of using literature in this way in a cross-curricular, literature-based family studies inquiry unit. In the balance of the chapter, I explain how that unit developed in our classroom over the course of a year.

Background

When I came to my school five years ago, I began working with intermediate kids and became aware of a disturbing fact: my grade-five students were not reading books. They would read whatever was necessary to complete work in the classroom—for example, directions and worksheets. Yet even when given a textbook assignment, they would superficially scan the page. I wanted to learn the answers to two questions:

1. Why are my students refusing to read books?
2. What can I do to change this?

I felt that getting my students into books was the single most important thing I could do. But how was I to do that?

I asked other teachers in the school how students could reach the ages of eleven and twelve and not appreciate books. The theories I was given ranged from too much television to "problematic" family situations. I considered these possible explanations.

Although children certainly tend to watch a great deal of television, and many of my students did live in difficult family settings, these are areas of life over which a teacher lacks control. These reasons seemed to blame the home, instead of building on what children bring to school. I decided to look at how I approached reading in my classroom and ask myself if my reading instruction supported a love of books.

I felt that, at least to some degree, it did. I read aloud to my students. I introduced authors. I required outside reading. I placed books around the room. But some of my methods did not support a love of reading. I demanded that book reports be written. I insisted that the students read books I considered "good," but that seemed dated to them. I was not familiar with enough current children's literature to match books to my students' interests and reading ability. I expected them to read books independently that were far too challenging.

I also looked at what students in my classroom were using for reading instruction. They were reading the basal. Some were reading a fifth-grade basal, some were still in the fourth-grade reader, and some were reading at lower levels. Week after week we read short stories from these books, contrived stories designed primarily to teach vocabulary and the structure of language. I knew my approach to books and the teaching of reading needed to change. But how?

Now I had a basic question, and I began to explore. I heard about literature-based curriculum. I wondered what that meant. I heard that some intermediate teachers were embracing the concept of whole language. I attended some workshops and conferences as a first step in gaining some rudimentary knowledge. As a result of what I learned in various sessions, I formulated a plan to change my classroom in two areas.

First, I made a decision to use "real" books as the foundation for all areas of study in my classroom. The reading of such books would be integrated in a systematic way into each topic or theme study.

Lee Galda (1988) discusses the importance of real books in the acquisition of literacy. She speaks of how the words and language in even the simplest of children's books is better than the writing in school reading texts. I also feel that the physical act of holding a real storybook, opening and closing a trade book, and carrying a book to one's desk for that day's reading and thinking are vital steps in developing lifelong readers. In addition, having a room filled with trade books where the emphasis is on good stories and finding appropriate books for one's own purposes rather than focusing on level of difficulty could erase lines of ability grouping, thus enabling all children to see themselves as readers. (Of course, I would continue to help students develop the strategies they need to become fluent readers.)

The second area I wanted to explore went beyond simply having good books in my classroom. I thought back to my own childhood, when I read every book in the library about women moving west. I remember reading whole books at one sitting. Why did I do that? What was there about that topic that drew me in? I believe there was something about the endurance of those women that held a connection for me. Galda (1988) says that texts only "live" when read by a person in a particular context. I began searching for ways to help students connect—ways to make the text live for them, to speak to their personal experiences and interests.

For the next two years I explored these two areas: using real and wonderful books in the classroom in place of the basal and studying the theory associated with children's response to literature. I familiarized myself with the latest in children's books and authors. I studied, through professional reading and classes, reader response theory and the use of inquiry-based themes. I became part of a study group where teachers from my school gathered together to discuss theory and practice. I used text sets, multiple copies, genre studies, and author studies as ways to organize real books in my classroom and make them more meaningful to my students. I incorporated response strategies (Harste, Short, and Burke 1988) and literature discussion groups to encourage reflection, interaction, and connection. It worked: my students showed obvious growth in their appreciation for books. Each new year, however, was a struggle and a challenge as I continually sought better ways to support students in making connections to literature and to the larger world.

During this period of searching I discovered the works of Eliot Wigginton. His book *Sometimes a Shining Moment: The Fox-fire Experience* (1985) related to my own desire to look at connections between life inside and outside the school. I was impressed with how Wigginton's students took ownership of their learning when they were encouraged to engage in activities that would help them understand their culture and community. They willingly engaged in tasks that promoted extensive reading and writing when these tasks allowed them to explore their own roots.

I considered my own classroom, where the students are Native American, African American, Mexican American, and European American. The school receives money from the government for special projects because half of our students fit the characteristics of potential high school dropouts. We are given special funding in order to find ways to keep these children in school. I thought about how I undertook the teaching of ethnic culture. Each ethnic group tended to be studied in isolation, either as a theme study, or as a "center" in the room, or perhaps in a special month. As a result, ethnicity appeared to be static and uniform rather than a dynamic feature of the living children in the room.

I could not recall the students ever making a personal response to any of these lessons. There had never been any occasion of powerful classroom sharing. Why would students want to stay in school through high school graduation when they had to leave who they were outside my classroom door? Why stay with school for years when it seems unreal and irrelevant and does not address the struggles and complexities of your own culture?

I began to wonder: If I provided more support in the classroom to help these students understand their roots and therefore understand themselves, would this invite connections to literature and one another in a more authentic, energetic way? In such a setting, the students themselves would become the curriculum.

I developed plans for a cross-curricular, literature-based family studies inquiry (see Figure 5–1). The inquiry began with the students getting to know one another in the classroom and then moved to the family. As the study progressed, I kept a personal journal and many artifacts. I made audio- and videotapes of discussions and took field notes. Figure 5–2 shows what happened over the course of the year as I attempted to follow the interest and energy of the students and to negotiate the curricular plan with them.

Getting to Know Each Other

When the students came into the classroom in the fall, my primary concern was to build a sense of community and lay the foundation for the family stories I hoped to generate later. We

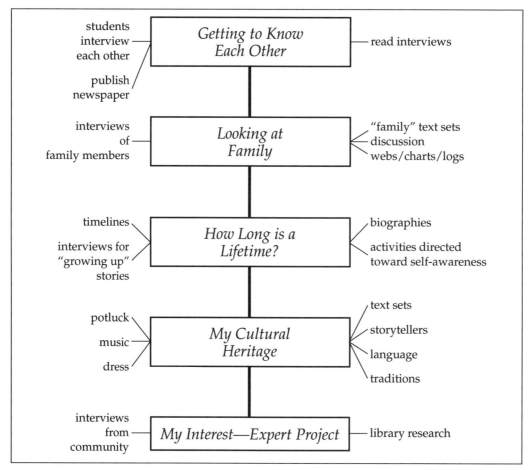

Figure 5–1
Thinking Ahead—Planning to Plan

began with a study of the interview process. Our reading program consisted of reading interviews in newspapers and magazines. Homework was to watch television interviews and write down the questions the interviewer asked. We talked about the importance of keeping the purpose of the interview in mind, and how to ask probing questions. The students then interviewed each other and published their interviews in a class newspaper. The interview became an integral part of our class work throughout the school year. At one point, a storyteller came to visit and was surprised to find a simulation of a television studio set where he was to be interviewed regarding his life as a storyteller.

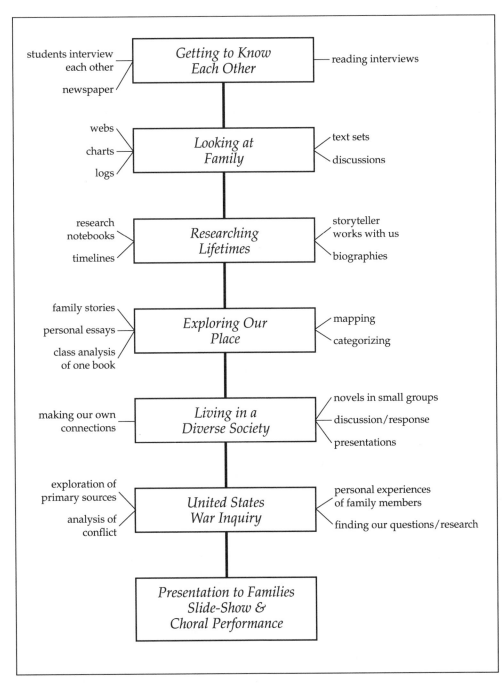

Figure 5–2
The Year Unfolds —Developing Curriculum with Students

Looking at Family

To support my beliefs that classroom studies need a strong literature component, I put together sets of text related to the topic of family. There were specific text sets on fathers, mothers, brothers and sisters, grandparents, and family stories from a storyteller's point of view. The text sets (Harste, Short, and Burke 1988) were made up of short pieces of reading material—primarily picture books with high-level concepts and poetry. Within the text set, a variety of ethnic backgrounds were represented. I arranged these materials in baskets and rotated them through small groups of children for browsing. My fifth graders became engrossed in them. Each group of students chose one set of books to reread and to discuss. These discussions quickly became a sharing of their own family stories. One group of five boys were examining the books on grandparents. One student told the story of how his grandfather died and how his life would never be quite the same. The other students had great empathy with him. It was touching to hear a group of such young people share an understanding of grief with each other:

BRIAN: My grandpa used to take us fishing in Pinetop. We did a lot of stuff like that with him. He died and we don't do that stuff . . . well, sometimes we do things like that and fish, but we . . . well, I miss him.

ERWIN: I just wish I could have done things with my grandfather. I wish I knew stories that my grandfather would have told me.

DAMIAN: Me, too. Brian, you were lucky. I will have to wait and see if my grandfather will tell me stories in heaven. But it is still sad for you.

In a later discussion with this same group, a Gila River Pima student referred to the book *Knots on a Counting Rope* (Martin and Archambault 1987). He expressed his wish to be an eagle dancer as his grandfather had been. He had lost his prior self-consciousness about being only one of two Native Americans in the class and spoke of his customs. These were the connections I was hoping would emerge.

The students kept literature response logs and often continued their thoughts in this log or commented on the stories other members of the group had shared. I encouraged them to write down their stories, and we soon had a folder of family stories. I suggested they take their knowledge of interviewing and their interest in family stories and ask members of their family to tell "I remember . . ." stories. Their writing then became a true journey from experience to paper. A folder of family stories was then begun, and as we worked our way through the year, each student added different kinds of written material (for example, original poems and research) to this folder.

To demonstrate good sharing and discussion, I also read books aloud to the students and encouraged responses in whole class discussion. One such discussion centered around the book *Pueblo Boy* (Keegan 1991). The topic arose as to how various cultures have celebrations. My Mexican American students thought their *folklorico* was similar to Native American dances. The Native Americans agreed that both kinds of dances were colorful, but that some Native American dances could be viewed as a kind of prayer. I saw this discussion of ethnic diversity as authentic sharing that promotes true understanding and respect.

I also encouraged group discussion centered on student writing. Sometimes students were asked questions by other students about aspects of their culture that they could not answer. For example, after a student shared a family story entitled "I Remember Making Christmas Tamales with My Grandmother," she was asked why Mexican Americans eat tamales at Christmas. The question encouraged her to look deeper into her own ethnicity.

Researching Lifetimes ❩

Since the students often shared stories of when they were younger, it seemed appropriate to work on time lines. Each child created a time line for a decade—the average length of their lives. Although they could list many experiences on this time line, I asked them to pick what they felt were the ten most significant and write a short paragraph about each one. Some may find it surprising that they did not list birthday parties or Christmas presents. They wrote about pets, and grandparents, and moving, and getting hurt or sick. Christina wrote about the first time she went fishing: "Because I caught my first fish I was proud of myself."

While we worked on our time lines we read biographies, reading and discussing the lives of famous people. I brought many books into the room for students to choose from; again, a diversity of cultures was represented. Although each student read a different biography, they met in groups for discussion. It seemed appropriate that after having examined our own lives so carefully, we should look at the lives of others and take the next step of looking at the contributions one can make over a lifetime.

After students chose a biography they were most interested in, they broke into groups for discussion. We had six groups: people who were authors, people in conflict, famous historical figures, people of great courage, western heroes, and creative people. In groups, the students discovered the commonalities across their books and drew some conclusions as to what made these people who they were. The final discussion centered on the lessons of life we could personally connect with from our book: "What is it about the life of this special person that holds a lesson for me?"

In one instance a student read a collection of stories about famous American Indian chiefs. He felt he should be in the group reading lives of western heroes. An interesting few days followed as the group grappled with the concept of what constitutes a hero. I heard powerful discussion as various viewpoints were considered.

We made a class time line and put all of the people we were reading about in their place in time. This took us back many years. During read-aloud, I read chapters from biography collections such as *Mathematicians Are People, Too* (Reimer and Reimer 1990), and we added these people to our time line. One student discovered that she was related to one of the people on our time line. She brought in a family history chart for proof.

The class then decided to do a "century" time line and research their own families back one hundred years. Again, they noted the ten most special events. In researching their stories, students often learned the history of their family's move from Mexico. One student was amazed to discover that a road near our school had been named for his family. Many of the family stories were connected to remembered events in American history, such as the sinking of the *Titanic* or the assassination of a president, which in turn led students to personal inquiries about these events. We often didn't have enough hours in the day to share all the stories.

Exploring Our Place }

About this time, I went to a local conference and was introduced to the book *My Place* (Wheatley and Rawlins 1989). This book tells about life in Australia by looking at one place and telling its story every ten years back in time, complete with maps so children can compare the changes. There is a tree in the center of all the maps; in the end there is only the tree.

I obtained several copies of the book. Each day we read two stories and examined the map for changes. Fortunately, whole language classrooms allow for spontaneity, because this book sent us spiraling off from my original plan for about six weeks. I kept careful records of each day's discussion. When the book was finished, we organized our book discussion topics into six categories: the pets children had through the years, the way children used the tree, the connections to events in broader society, Australian terms, the family history throughout the book, and the jobs people had through the years. The students then formed groups to revisit the book and take notes on their particular topic. The class was eager to share the book with others, so we organized in a visual way the information we had collected and put it on display in the library. The group looking at pets made a bar graph with pictures of animals to illustrate how many pets were dogs, how many were cats, and so forth. Each block on the graph represented a certain year. Another group made a big tree and drew all the ways the tree was used, with each large leaf representing a year. These projects were wonderful examples of collecting, organizing, and sharing information—as well as demonstrations of authentic response to a piece of literature.

There was more to come. On Monday morning after the projects were done, a student brought in a "My Place" of her own. She had drawn a rough map of her neighborhood and highlighted the places that were of importance to her. She had a short essay about her pets, and her family and their jobs. She included her picture. We all thought it was a great idea and spent the next week making our own maps and telling about our place in time. Kristen wrote a particularly poignant essay. "This is my place where I live with my mother," it began. "My Dad doesn't live here any more. He lives at his place." Whether or not Kristen realized it, she had touched on the very topic the class had called "connections to broader society." Many students in the class shared this kind of extended family.

Through Kristen's example and as part of the family studies inquiry, students had a safe place to share their family situations. I began to think more broadly about my definition of culture. I felt that consideration must be given to the issues *all* my students must face. I came to understand that culture goes beyond ethnicity; it incorporates the ways in which we live and think in the world. One of the cultures I began to think about was the culture of generations and the differences between my adult culture and their kid culture.

Living in a Diverse Society

For the next literature experience relating to the family studies inquiry, I chose a variety of novels from which students could select. Five students would read the same novel and discuss it together. I wanted to use books that had a strong family theme and that also represented a variety of cultures. I found *Racing the Sun* (Pitts 1988), *Maniac Magee* (Spinelli 1991), and *A Jar of Dreams* (Uchida 1981) to be especially effective. In these discussions, a range of topics, such as homelessness and attitudes toward old age, arose. The following is an excerpt from one session in which the ethnic aspect of culture was under discussion. The book that served as the focus for the discussion was *Racing the Sun* (Pitts 1988). The students are all boys. Brian is European American, Tekoa is African American, Erwin is Gila River Pima, and Ronald and Damian are Mexican American. The boys are discussing why the father in the story (a Navajo who is a college professor) does not wish to return to the reservation to visit the grandfather, who is ill.

BRIAN: Sometimes people aren't proud of their heritage because the traditions seem silly.

RONALD: It doesn't seem up to date. The book calls it the "old ways."

BRIAN: The father was just trying to get away from the stereotyping of Indians—you know, riding horses, shooting arrows . . .

DAMIAN: He probably didn't remember the language, either.

ERWIN: I think people should stay in their heritage, but no one in my family is into it. Like the guy in the story, they want to go with life and pretend they are not Indian. I feel like Brandon—I'm interested.

TEKOA: I'm like Brandon, too. I want to remember.

ERWIN: I think if I was Tekoa I would get mad at the way they treated the blacks—as slaves and all. Some people still treat them as long ago—as slaves—you have to get to know black people . . .

TEKOA: Indians were treated badly, too.

BRIAN: They had to prove they were equal to white culture before we could talk about the heritage. I think we should study all cultures because they all have important people . . . like Martin Luther King . . .

ERWIN: And Malcolm X.

Once again literature provided the vehicle for students from several cultural backgrounds to share a common ground as they explored their personal beliefs and experiences. They were able to share from the heart and to support one another. This can lead to mutual respect and true understanding in the classroom.

Going on from There

During the time we were working on our family studies inquiry, we studied American history more formally, primarily through the use of the textbook. Many of the family stories shared by the students related to events in American history, particularly wars. The students therefore elected to finish the year with a war inquiry. They worked in groups to study the Revolutionary War, the Civil War, World War I, World War II, and the Vietnam conflict. Using their interviewing expertise, they taped interviews with family and community members. When appropriate, we went to the library to read newspaper articles from the time period. Students brought family artifacts into the room, including pictures, old uniforms, and medals. Throughout, we studied people in conflict. Family and cultural diversity were the touchstones to which the discussion always returned.

Summary

When the school year ended, I reviewed all the data I had collected. I had stacks of writing, transcripts of discussions, and the various projects the children had created. As I began to dig deeper into this material, I came to see that, given a supportive environment, children would get to know one another and become interested in the variety of perspectives that we have, our own particular view of the world. The children in my class wanted to explore many differences, not only those of cultural heritage, but also those aspects of "kid culture" that concern them deeply, such as the clothes we choose to wear and the messages that clothing conveys.

American history had become more real for my students because history was now not just dates from a textbook, but people and families. They also seemed to better understand time, as we added people and events to various time lines throughout the year. Finally, I believe that all the children came away from the class with a greater sense of themselves. Our classroom had become a place where home and school merged.

It was not always easy. The students, accustomed to simply answering questions, needed a lot of support in learning how to respond to books. They had to build a trust in their classmates and understand that I, also, truly valued their responses—and that there really was no one right answer.

It was difficult at times to be a researcher. Taking field notes of discussions or using video- or audiotapes was time-consuming and awkward. I sometimes felt in the beginning that perhaps it wouldn't happen—maybe the students would not connect with these books in the ways I had hoped. In addition, many projects took longer than I had anticipated. Nevertheless, in the end, we had a powerful, energetic study. It concluded with a presentation to parents on the last day of school. The class sang a medley of songs related to families. As I looked at each face, together representing many cultures, I thought to myself, "E pluribus unum—Out of many, one."

6

SHEILA HOFSTEDT

Learning that Keeps on Going: The Power of Literature in Social Studies

O NE OF THE QUESTIONS TEACHERS OFTEN ASK THEM-
selves is "My students may be enjoying this unit now, but what
will be the long-term outcome?" When Danny Clark, a student
in my fifth-grade class, wrote his response to Jim Murphy's *The
Boys' War* (1990), I became reassured about the long-term outcome in my class.

> I was really curious as to why the Union would allow musicians of any age
> to go. Because, I mean what if another army made a surprise attack on them
> and the little drummer boy or bugler boy got killed. They would be much
> too young to die. And it would be the Union's fault if the little boy got killed
> because they were the ones who allowed young musicians in the first place.

Units of study about the Civil War are typical for the fifth-
grade curriculum. I wanted to do something other than a "textbook only" approach. I wanted my students to learn about the
Civil War from multiple sources and perspectives. I wanted
them to read a variety of viewpoints and to become comfortable
in formulating their own views. I hoped their opinions would
change and evolve through discussion. I wanted to provide the
opportunity for them to learn history in a meaningful and
developmentally appropriate way. I wanted my students to
realize that war, like life, is not a black and white issue, and that
there are often more than two sides to any issue.

In the course of our six-week interdisciplinary unit, I asked
the students to read and think about nonfiction and fiction
books that interested them rather than to memorize names,
dates, and places. We used the textbook chapters as outlines,
just the beginning of our study. The nonfiction reading provided information, while the historical fiction touched the emotional and personal side of each child. Discussion and written
work deepened understanding. Projects at the end of the study
helped students synthesize the entire unit.

Focusing the Unit

Although the content of our sessions varied, we followed a
regular routine throughout the six weeks of the study. The students had one-hour work sessions four times a week. I also
scheduled read-aloud sessions for half an hour every day.
Before I established this routine, I placed nonfiction selections

on a front-facing bookshelf (a discarded grocery store magazine rack). I used personal and public library books to attract the students' interest to the topic. Some students brought books from home to display as well.

I began the unit with the KWL (Know, Want to know, Learned) method. I asked students, "What do you know about the Civil War?" I recorded their responses, just as they said them, on a large piece of paper and posted it in the room. Next I asked, "What do you want to learn about the Civil War?" I followed the same procedure. However, this time, I left space between the questions for students to write in answers as they read.

Then I assigned the social studies textbook chapters about the Civil War. From prior classroom experiences, some of my students had been accustomed to working out of textbooks. Rather than assigning the recall questions at the end of each section, I assigned the "Ideas to Discuss" portion. I had the students write their answers down. During our first work sessions, the children read and wrote from the text. These sessions were followed by a discussion session where I encouraged the students to share their ideas from their written responses.

Our first fiction read-aloud was Joyce Hansen's *Which Way Freedom?* (1986). The students became so interested in the book, I continued with the sequel, *Out from this Place* (Hansen 1988). Both are superb historical novels about the experiences of three black slaves. The Fort Pillow, Tennessee, Massacre and the settling of the Sea Islands by former slaves frame these moving, well-written books. In our read-aloud sessions, I read for twenty minutes and we then discussed the book for about ten minutes. During the discussions, I modeled thinking questions that I would expect the students to be able to use later in their small literature discussion groups.

The Work Sessions

I began each of our one-hour work sessions with a nonfiction read-aloud. The remaining thirty minutes were spent in individual reading and recording or small-group discussion.

Delia Ray's *A Nation Torn* (1990) and Ina Chang's *A Separate Battle* (1991) were two powerful nonfiction read-alouds. *A Nation Torn* provided a great deal of background information on the turmoil that led to the war. Chapters from Chang's book and newspaper and magazine articles that focused on the experiences of women and minorities expanded the study. I was able to find an article on Tejano soldiers during the war. Many of my students identified with the Tejano soldiers. In general, students appreciated learning about the roles people of their own sex or ethnic group played in the war.

I began our first work session following our work in the textbook with a brief book talk on each of the nonfiction books that had been on display. I asked each student to select a different book. To facilitate the selection of books, I randomly drew name cards. As I drew each name, that student would select his or her book. I allowed students to negotiate and trade books. I also established a classroom checkout procedure. Students were expected to do some of their reading outside of school as homework.

When each student was satisfied with his or her book selection, we made our learning logs—ten sheets of loose-leaf paper stapled inside a construction paper cover. On the front, students wrote their name and the name of the book they were reading, leaving room to add other titles as needed. Each day, students were to record the book title, date, and number of pages read at the top of the page. The remainder of the page was then roughly divided into thirds. The three sections were labeled "Learning," "Questions," and "Responses." I stressed that the most important section should be the Response section.

During or near the end of a reading period in our work sessions, I asked students to write in their learning logs. Students accustomed to primarily textbook work needed extra help with this. I read aloud thoughtful student responses daily, at first. Responses such as Danny's quoted at the beginning of this chapter prompted other students to think more deeply about their books and beliefs.

The Literature Studies

About the tenth day of our unit, when most of the students were finishing reading their nonfiction texts, I began to bring in historical fiction. As I had done with the nonfiction, I brought the books in and gave the students some days in which to browse before making selections. Once again I utilized the public library in order to get multiple copies of each of the titles I offered. I selected books based on their content, the appropriate reading level for fifth grade, and availability. The students were offered the following books for their literature studies:

Charley Skedaddle by Patricia Beatty (Morrow, 1987)
Turn Homeward, Hannalee by Patricia Beatty (Morrow, 1984)
Who Comes with Cannons? by Patricia Beatty (Morrow, 1992)
The Tamarack Tree by Patricia Clapp (Lothrop, 1986)
A Month of Seven Days by Shirley Climo (HarperCollins, 1987)
Shades of Gray by Carolyn Reeder (Avon, 1989)
The Perilous Road by William O. Steele (Scholastic, 1958)

On day eleven, I read the book jacket blurbs aloud to the class. I established a criteria for self-selection of the books. I asked the students to consider their interest level in the book, the writing style of the book, and the reading level of the book. I encouraged the students to peruse and read the first few pages of each book over a couple of days. Finally, I asked each student to rank order the books.

I did not want to assign the books. Instead, I created a large chart that listed each title with five spaces below. Students drew numbers, then signed up for their choice when their number was called. I had more spaces than students so that no one was left without some choice.

Using our established checkout procedure, students took their books and met in groups. The first task of each group was to decide how many pages to read each night in order to finish the book by the date due, two weeks away. They were also to determine a leader for each of their five discussion sessions, which would occur every other day. The days in between were used for additional reading and, later, project work.

I supplied a daily schedule sheet that I adapted from an article I had read in *The Reading Teacher* (Bath 1992). Each student created a literature study log similar to the learning logs. However, their literature study logs included the daily schedule sheet at the front and another sheet of open-ended literature discussion questions at the back. I felt it was important for there to be specific guidelines for behavior and expectations within the literature groups (see Figure 6–1). This was the first experience working in

WHEN YOU ARE THE LEADER:

1. Read your section *thoroughly,* marking passages that you want to discuss with a Post-it note.

2. Develop *thinking* questions (7–10).

3. Plan a written assignment that has value.

4. Involve *everyone* in your group.

5. Don't evaluate individual answers.

6. Remember: you are helping them to think about the story; your job is to facilitate a good discussion that involves everyone!

WHEN YOU ARE NOT THE LEADER:

1. Keep up with all assignments.

2. Think about the social/task goals.

3. Be respectful of the leader and fellow members.

4. Take an active part.

Session 1 Leader _____ Pages _____

Session 2 Leader _____ Pages _____

Session 3 Leader _____ Pages _____

Session 4 Leader _____ Pages _____

Session 5 Leader _____ Pages _____

Figure 6–1
Daily Schedule for Literature Groups

this way for many of the students, but it was very successful. Students took their roles as leaders and participants very seriously.

Ashley Kelly's group was reading *The Tamarack Tree* (Clapp 1986). One of the leader's questions was "How have some of the other characters changed throughout this book?" After the discussion, all the students were assigned to write their personal responses to that question in their literature response logs. Ashley wrote,

> Another opinion change that Rosemary went through is which side (the North or the South) she wanted to win the war. In the beginning she liked what the North was fighting for (according to the *Citizen*) and she liked Abe Lincoln. But once the war got closer and the North even ruined their house, Rosemary wanted the South to win, more than the North.

As leader, Chris Gates assigned his group the task of writing a letter to the main character in *The Perilous Road* (Steele 1958) to tell him how they felt about his brother joining the Union army. Katja Rivera wrote,

> I think your brother was kind of right and kind of wrong in joining the Union army. I think he is right because he has his opinion on things, and he believes in joining the army, so he should. I think he is against slavery, so he should fight against slavery.
>
> I also think he's wrong because it's kind of weird fighting against your home, family, etc. But I think you should let him do what he wants to. You are for the South, nobody says anything about it. So I think you should be more fair to your brother.

Once the historical fiction literature study groups had gotten under way, we took one session to brainstorm a list of possible projects. I encouraged projects that would expand both the presenter's and the audience's understanding of the books. Our idea list included skits, readers' theater, talk shows, murals, mobiles of objects found in the book, and picture books of descriptive phrases from the book. I discussed with the students my goal that the purpose of the projects be to deepen their understanding of the novel and encouraged them to continue to discuss the book while they worked.

We used another session to develop an evaluation of the projects. I facilitated this process by leading a discussion of the requirements of a good project. We talked abut the importance of practicing the introduction and giving a brief synopsis of the book as part of the presentation. We agreed that it would be more valuable to have evaluations that required specific comments rather than simply grades. The students also felt it would be important for the evaluations to be anonymous and to be shared with each group on the same day they presented. I typed our evaluation form and made copies available for use during the creation of the projects, as well as on the days of the presentations.

Broadening Our Experiences

The students were so excited by the two books by Joyce Hansen I read to them that some of them elected to write a letter to the author. She wrote back! The students were thrilled to be among the first to know that she was at work on a third book, a sequel to the two we'd read together.

I contacted a local group that does Civil War reenactments. The participants each create historically accurate characters whom they present to others. We invited one member to our class. The students loved the experience. More important, the depth of their response and their questions so impressed our presenter that she told the students that they were one of the most intelligent groups she'd ever spoken to.

Toward the end of our study, when all of the groups had finished their reading, we returned to our original KWL charts. We looked at what we had known in the beginning and reevaluated the accuracy of our former knowledge. We revised as needed. We discussed the answer to the questions that had been listed and shared other learning that had occurred outside of our original questions.

Finally, we created a "cause and effect" diagram. I drew a rectangle on a large piece of paper. I wrote the words "Civil War" in the center of the box. I then drew horizontal lines going in and coming out of the rectangle. We wrote the causes of the Civil War on the incoming lines, and effects the war had on our country on the outgoing lines. In the course of this discussion the vast knowledge the students had acquired throughout our unit became apparent.

Yes, But Did They Really Learn?

Nine months after the presentation of projects, during the course of writing this chapter, I decided to try, at least informally, to answer the question suggested at the beginning of this chapter. How much did they really learn? I phoned my former students and asked them which aspects of the study stood out in their memory, as well as how this unit compared to a "textbook only" approach.

David Meilleur had this to say: "Reading historical fiction and working in groups was a lot of fun because it gave you a chance to discuss the book with kids who were reading the same book and were at the same point as you were." Comparing it to the textbook-only approach, he stated, "It was a lot more interactive because you got more into the era by reading about how other people (not just famous people) had to cope with the war, and with life during the war."

Ashley Kelly commented, "My biggest memory was reading books instead of textbooks. [It] put a big impression on you. You could really tell how things were in a fiction book rather than out of a textbook." Comparing nonfiction books to a textbook, she said, "You got a lot of facts, but not just the basic view, you got to the point. You actually got to look into what interested you." She continued, "I loved the projects; you got to show what you learned, not just answer a question from a textbook."

Emily Kuchar summarized in this way: "I got to see the South's point of view . . . not just that the North were the good guys and the South were the bad guys. . . . I learned a lot more this way. With a textbook, you read it, then you forget about it. You answer four questions and it's over. This just kind of kept on going."

Learning that "keeps on going" is the source of that inner satisfaction we all seek as teachers. And that is what keeps us motivated and committed to our work year in, year out.

Throughout this Civil War unit, I acknowledged the background information students brought to the study. I allowed for choice in the resources used. I set up frameworks that encouraged thoughtful responses and provided opportunities for students to learn and discuss their learning in small groups as well as with the whole class. Facilitating our study in this way did not just make the unit fun. It enabled the children to invest in their own lifelong learning, and that made all the difference.

MEEGAN I. GLINER

Theme Cycles Through the Eyes of a Student Teacher

*H*AVING JUST FINISHED THE CREDENTIAL COURSES AT MY university, I was anxious to put into practice what I had learned. The works of Nancie Atwell (1987) and Linda Rief (1992) inspired me. I, too, wanted to teach as they did, to have a learner-centered, process-oriented classroom. That meant, however, trying something that was new to me and not part of my own learning experiences.

My eight-week student teaching assignment was in a self-contained fifth-grade classroom. The students were from an upper-middle-income neighborhood and typically did well in school. Their grades were high, as were their achievement test scores. I believed that with these older elementary students, I would be able to try out the student-centered, integrated curriculum approach I had learned so much about in my methods courses. The students and I would be able to ask questions and discover the answers together, since the students were old enough to do the research and discovery themselves.

As the resident teacher and I began to plan the Native American unit I was to teach, I knew I didn't want to be stuck using just the textbook, even if it was new and up to date. During the first week of my placement, I attended an in-service along with classroom teachers on the newly adopted social studies textbooks. Everyone was excited; you could tell by the remarks they made as they looked through the new textbooks.

"Aren't the pictures beautiful?"

"There is so much information to cover."

"What a great new book, and so teachable."

"Look at all the ideas they give you. You won't have to plan anything, it's all right here for you."

I mentioned to my resident teacher that there were some methods I would like to try in addition to using the textbook. For example, before beginning a topic, I would like to have the students list what they already know and want to know. I suggested that the students might find it interesting to research their own questions and inquiries, rather than the ones prescribed by the textbook or the usual "Indian report." The resident teacher agreed, even though it wasn't the way he typically taught.

I would be allowed to let the students raise and research questions if I also followed the information in the textbook and had the students answer the questions at the end of the chapters.

With me, the students would demonstrate their learning through projects, presentations, and the research process. At the completion of the unit, the resident teacher required that the students write a traditional report following his outline. When I started our study of Native Americans, following the theme cycle approach (Edelsky, Altwerger, and Flores 1991), the resident teacher left me with complete responsibility for the classroom. At times I thought of turning back to the textbook, but I considered it worth the risk for myself and my students to try what I considered a more valuable learning experience.

First Day

After lunch, I came into the classroom with large pieces of paper, a handful of big markers, and a roll of masking tape. I taped two big pieces of paper on the front chalkboard. On one I wrote "What we know about Native Americans." On the other I wrote "What we want to know about Native Americans." The students just looked at me, not really sure what I was doing. So I asked them the question:

"What do you know about Native Americans?"

No response.

"Anything! Tell me anything you know, anything at all."

"Can I look in the textbook?"

"Not right now. Just tell me anything you know. Maybe something you learned last year, something you remember from a project you did, anything."

Again, silence.

But then, slowly, hands started going up. They were tentative at first, not sure if what they said would be shot down as wrong, incorrect, or dumb.

STUDENT: They were the first people to live in America.

ME: Okay. What else?

STUDENT: They made tents from animals.

STUDENT: Yeah! And they used all parts of the animals.

ME: Now, are we sure that all Native Americans made tents from animals?

STUDENT: No. But some did.

ME: Yes, some did. So, let's just say, "Some Native Americans used animals."

Again silence. Perhaps they had started to feel that there are right and wrong answers. I changed my approach.

ME: Remember, anything you say is valid. I will write it all down. Later, we'll decide if these facts are true when we decide what we want to know. But for now, just tell me everything you can about what you know right now.

And so it started to flow, until students began sharing a tremendous amount of information they didn't even know they knew.

STUDENT: They use what they have. . . .

STUDENT: They make things from natural resources.

STUDENT: They moved a lot.

STUDENT: Some were fighters. . . .

STUDENT: Some were slaves. . . .

STUDENT: There are chiefs.

STUDENT: They had customs. . . .

STUDENT: Rites. . . .

STUDENT: Traditions.

When our chart paper was full, as shown in Figure 7–1, I stopped. Hands were still in the air, wanting to tell me more. For a moment, I was in awe. "Hold your thoughts," I said. "I know you still know more, but for now, keep it in your head and look at all the facts we have written now. Did you ever realize you knew so much? What would be the point of my teaching you all this information if you already know it? What I would like you to do now is tell me what you want to know. If you could ask any question about Native Americans, what would it be?"

Again, silence.

Then, it started. One by one, the hands went up with questions about things I never would have thought to teach.

STUDENT: Who are they?

STUDENT: Do they all have two names? [This question came from a student who remembered that in *Island of the Blue Dolphins* (O'Dell 1978), Karina

---

the first people to live in America

some made tents out of animals
    they use all parts of the animals

use what they had, things from natural resources
    kill only what they need

they moved a lot

some were slaves

have chiefs

customs, rites, traditions

live in tribes

some wore feathers

wear little amounts of clothing

make pots, baskets

weapons made with obsidian, bows from rib bones

killed people with tomahawks
    scalping started with the French

use tules for boats, carved boats from wood

hunt their own food

some were fighters, wore face paint

some have sweat houses

Figure 7–1
What We Know
about Native
Americans

has two names. He wanted to know if all Native Americans employed this custom. I was amazed at the connections students were making.]

STUDENT: How did they get to America?

STUDENT: Where did they get their language?

STUDENT: How did they distinguish what land belongs to which group?

And as always, the fun questions that every child wants to ask. No censoring was allowed, so the questions kept coming.

STUDENT: What do they do for fun?

STUDENT: How are weapons made?

Finally, we had to stop. (The finished list is shown in Figure 7–2.) We had run out of time. We ended the class period excited and motivated.

Figure 7–2
What We
Want to Know
about Native
Americans

Who are they?

Do all Native Americans have two names? Why?

How did they get to America?
   Where did they come from?

How did they get their language? How did it start?

How do they distinguish what land belonged to which tribe?

What do they do for entertainment?

How do they make their baskets?

How do they keep their food fresh?

How do they make weapons?
   Did they copy it or make it up? Who did they copy from?
   Did they trade or make weapons?

How do they put face paint on? Why?
   Where do they get the colors?

How do they sharpen their knives?

Who made up sweat houses?

How are chiefs chosen?

What are houses made of?

The Next Week

Because of the class schedule it was the end of the next week before we had time to continue our theme cycle.

At the teacher's request, we would address the questions in view of specific Native American people. I asked the students to name the people they wanted to know about. They asked if they could look in their textbook or encyclopedia for names, and I said, "Definitely!" After we made our list they broke into groups based on the people they were interested in knowing more about. Some groups had six people, some only two. But they were all in a group they were most interested in, not one I had picked out. I handed out papers and markers for the students to copy the questions they wanted to research from our whole class question list. The next step was to answer the questions.

"What if it's not on the class paper on the board?"

"Write it down anyway. This is your chance to ask anything you want. Don't censor anything anyone says. Just write it down. Maybe you'll decide to research it, and maybe you won't."

The groups were buzzing with questions. The group leaders were writing, frantically trying to keep up with group members' inquiries. I roamed the room reassuring them that yes, that is an excellent question, or yes, you can ask that, or no, that is not a dumb question. For example, students studying the Ohlone did not care so much about where they were from, but they did want to know about how they lived, whether they made baskets and jewelry from beads, and how and where they obtained their food (Figure 7–3). These were their questions, not mine.

"Can we start looking for answers?" I turned around on hearing the question. Some students were already heading for encyclopedias and textbooks to find the answers to their questions.

"Well, I wasn't planning on starting this today, but since you're interested, yes, you may start researching. I brought in some books. They're on the front table." As soon as I said that, students charged the table. The night before, I had raided my

---

WHAT WE WANT TO KNOW ABOUT THE OHLONE TRIBE

   Keeping food fresh

   Beads

   Baskets

   Chief

   Dances

   How to make tule boats

   Food supply

   Weapon use

   How is face paint made?

   Basket making

Figure 7–3
A Brainstorm List of Research Questions and Ideas from One Group

local public library for every book on Native Americans I could find—on Cherokees, Apaches, Aztecs, Ohlones, and more. Many students asked if they could go to their own libraries to find more books, and of course I approved. The next day, their desks were filled with books.

Weeks Three to Five

We were on a roll. For the next three weeks, the students met in their groups two or three times a week to research their questions, talk with group members, share information with each other. At this point, my job became that of observer, assistant, reassurer, encourager. I spent my time roaming between groups in the cafeteria (our new meeting place, since our classroom opened onto other classrooms and our talking and moving would disturb them), finding out where they were, what they needed help with, and what they felt like sharing with me.

Each group picked out a table in the cafeteria to be their meeting place. They could spread out their books, papers, and question sheets.

During these weeks we also talked about how to present their information to the class. I didn't want to limit them at the beginning with instruction on presentations. Once they had information, I felt, they could more easily decide how to present it, rather than vice versa.

The Ohlone group went to a local river to find materials similar to tules to make a model boat and baskets. The Hopi group was interested in the homes, clothing, and crafts of their tribe, so they decided to build a model village with clothing and pottery. The Aztec group researched the fighting and torture practices, as well as chiefs and tribal structure. They worked on a demonstration of punishment and built model weapons to show the class. Once they understood that anything was possible, they came up with all sorts of ideas for presentations; any amount of time I could give them was never enough. Imagine: students excitedly asking when we would be doing our work, rather than grumbling about social studies.

Presentations ❩

Finally, the week arrived when the students were to present their projects to the class. The class was excited. They wanted to know who was sharing on which day. They were ready, nervous, and enthusiastic to get started. For several weeks, they had been working very hard. They wanted to share all of the information they had found. They were proud of what they had done, and they had every right to be.

Every day, three groups were scheduled for presentations. They were given as much time as they needed. The Ohlone group, for example, decided to talk about the use of the tule plant for boat making. They spoke of the Ohlone's dependence on water for fish and transportation. This group also managed to cover information on the importance of the chief and the use of weapons for hunting and defense. What was most interesting about their presentation was that rather than just sharing their research by reading from a written report, they made models, drew pictures, and showed us evidence instead of just telling us about it.

Evaluations ❩

As I had explained to the students at the beginning, I would not be the one to grade their presentations. The entire class would have the opportunity to share input on how well the group did and what kind of effort they had made in the last few weeks.

Based on a model evaluation form used in one of my university methods courses, I developed an evaluation sheet. Every student would evaluate each group project as it was presented to the class. The form was a simple half page with the following statements and blank areas for them to fill in:

What I learned about from this presentation:
What I enjoyed most about this presentation:
If I had done this presentation, this is what I would have done differently:
I would give this group this grade: E S+ D S S– U

I explained to the class I would look at all the student evaluations, not just my own, in determining the grade.

Each student also received a self-evaluation form to assess their own learning. It was similar to the evaluation sheet they used for others, only the self-evaluation form was a full page, with more room for responses, and the question "Why?" at the end, following the grade they would give themselves. I found it enlightening to see what their reasons were ("I tried my best"; "I really learned a lot, and I did a lot of work"). An example of a completed self-evaluation form is shown in Figure 7–4.

Finally, at the end of each presentation, before the forms were collected, the audience shared remarks they had written down for the presenting group. They said such things as "I liked the pictures you drew of the village" or "I liked how you brought in real clothes and pottery" or "I liked how you shared a lot of information." They were also allowed to ask questions of the group, such as "How did you make the model town?" or "How did you make the weapons?" or "Where did you find that information?"

Once each group's evaluation forms were collected, I would assign the grade and meet with the group the next day to go over some highlights of what the class thought of their presentation. They were then allowed to keep the class evaluations for future reference. They wanted to know what their peers had learned from their presentation and were amazed at the variety of responses from their classmates. Most important, their evaluation meant more than a grade on a chapter test. It was not a notation on a piece of paper that they would take home, show their parents, and throw away. This was something they could hold onto. It showed that what they did meant something, because it was based on their own questions and interests, and it showed that they were able to share and learn with one another.

NATIVE AMERICAN   PRESENTATION:
SELF EVALUATION

Apache

What I learned most from my research and presentation:

I learned that the Apaches were afraid of ghosts and that they would do dances. ~~and~~ They made conees out of tules. There faces were painted with smashed berries. There from the Southwest.

What I enjoyed most about doing my research and presentation:

I enjoyed working with other people. ~~The~~ The Apache were interesting. The things they did were different than what other Indians do.

If I did this again, this is what I would do differently:

Well, I dont think I would do eany thing differently. Except that we wouldn't be able to bring in the same staff¿¿¿?(See?)

I would give myself this grade: (E) S+ S S- U

why? I would give myself a E because I worked hard. I helped get some of props. I worked out diffucalties between me and group members I offered a time when all the group members and I could get together at my house. Our group coparated!

Figure 7–4 Completed Self-Evaluation Form

Reflections

Even after the unit on Native Americans was completed, the students continued to ask questions. This proved to me that if students are given the opportunity, they can ask better questions and learn more than ever could be taught to them from a textbook. For the first time, they were allowed to raise the questions. No question from a textbook, no matter how well asked, can be as valuable as a question asked by a student.

As a result of the risks that we took together as a class, we all learned a great deal. The students experienced learning as a cooperative, rather than a competitive, act. They learned how to look critically at each other's work as well as their own, and give and take constructive criticism. Rather than relying on the teacher for the grade, they realized it was more important to learn for the sake of learning, and to expand their own knowledge and the knowledge of their classmates through their own interests, not the teacher's assignments. Most important, they learned to think, examine, and critically analyze information, books, articles, speakers. Instead of just accepting the facts on the page, they learned to delve deeper into the material to search for answers to their questions.

And what did I learn? I can't imagine reading aloud from a textbook, turning to page 57 simply because it's the next page in the textbook. I can't imagine standing in front of a room of thirty-six students and spitting out facts that will go in one ear and out the other. Having tried moving away from a teacher-centered, textbook-driven approach, I can't imagine ever teaching any other way.

Epilogue

I completed my eight-week placement before the winter break. After the break, I spoke with the resident teacher to see how the students were doing. The students had written the traditional reports, and he found them excellent.

Having completed the credential requirements, I am currently employed as a multigrade (sixth, seventh, and eighth) classroom teacher. The philosophy of the school is progressive. I was hired because the student-centered approach I learned in my credential courses fits the philosophy of the school.

By not accepting the status quo of social studies textbook teaching, I am even more prepared as a teacher, determined to implement good teaching. Looking at social studies through the students' eyes and minds seems to me the only logical way to teach. Reviewing the students' comments on the Native American theme cycle, I believe they agree:

"I learned a lot about the Ohlone, and I had hardly ever heard of them before."

"I enjoyed being with the people, doing my paper, and doing crafts."

"I liked learning about Pueblo Indians and I like sharing my discoveries about Pueblo Indians."

8

SUZANNE SOOHOO
BRENDA BROWN

Developing Voice in the Democratic Classroom

*The only way to prepare for democratic participation is to
create a community in which democracy is practiced each day.*
Kriesberg 1993, p. 29

*T*HE SETTING IS A FOURTH-GRADE PUBLIC CLASSROOM IN Cerritos, California. Cerritos is a suburban middle-class community twenty miles south of Los Angeles. Five years ago, it was named the most culturally diverse community in the nation by two national magazines. Of the twenty-six students in our class, there were six Chinese Americans, five Korean Americans, three Far East Indian Americans, one Filipino American, one Japanese American, four European-Americans, three Hispanic Americans, two African Americans, and one American Indian. Nine of the students were born and previously educated in a country other than the United States. The languages represented in the classroom were English, Mandarin, Cantonese, Korean, Gujurati, Urdu, and Spanish. With a diversity of customs and cultures, our challenge was to build a classroom community in which individual strengths and differences were respected and regularly celebrated. As part of this, we wanted to encourage students to build a democratic community. We believed we could develop a classroom in which students could actively participate in shaping classroom conditions, share power with the teacher, and have voice.

Both the classroom teacher, Brenda, and the university researcher, Suzanne, were particularly interested in students with unsung voices, the silent students who either chose to keep their thoughts to themselves or had not yet developed the language of social participation. We began the school year by introducing class meetings and the writing workshop as ways to create a community in which democracy could be practiced daily.

Class Meetings

Class meetings convened once a week. Students were invited to discuss their concerns about any aspect of learning or classroom life. Agenda items were mutually determined by the students and the teacher.

Early in the year, class meetings centered around mutual expectations of the role of student and the role of teacher. The students and the teacher expressed what they needed from each other in order to feel successful in school. Rules, roles, and responsibilities were suggested, tried, modified, or discarded as we sought to define the code of conduct for our community. For example, the children initially suggested the rule "Always raise your hand to speak." We soon found that this was too restrictive and didn't fit the dynamics of our interactions. Therefore, this rule was modified through class meetings to "Listen to each other."

Students told the teacher, Brenda, that they expected her to be fair. She expected them to be responsible. While this may sound like a simple exchange in establishing classroom conditions, it also generated several days of discussion as we fleshed out what fairness and responsibility meant. Through these discussions children realized that each of our roles could be negotiated. For many, this was a completely new experience.

Brenda followed these discussions by suggesting we create a simulated workplace in the classroom. The children agreed that classroom jobs and working relationships would be fun and would demonstrate student responsibility. Roles were mutually defined at class meetings, and an open application process was instituted. Jobs varied from a personnel manager to a banker to a real estate manager who was responsible for collecting "rent" from each student for the use of their desks. In addition, an economic system was put in place and students earned wages in the form of play money.

The role holding the most responsibility in the simulated workplace was general manager. The general manager not only had to monitor all the jobs in the classroom, but also had to select the best qualified candidates from applications to fill open jobs, using a criterion of fairness. Fairness also influenced how the general manager handled the responsibility of hearing student grievances. These grievances generally targeted what students perceived as unpleasant work conditions, such as complaints about "the boss"—that is, the teacher.

Issues from our workplace community became a rich source of class meeting discussions. One example focused on equability. Should jobs with more responsibility get more compensation? The general manager, students agreed, should be paid double since his or her grand responsibility was to monitor all class jobs.

Through class meetings, students were also responsible for making decisions about instruction. For example, when is group work the most effective approach to studying? If we chose group work, how should groups be made up? How should groups be graded? How should the individual be graded? Initially, students set up their groups by merely selecting their friends. The teacher was to act as mediator and not usurp the power of the group. This wasn't always easy. On more than one occasion, it was necessary to let groups of "best friends" learn that friendship was not necessarily the best criterion of a good working relationship. Because all groups were asked to work collaboratively, students soon realized the importance of recruiting some "experts" to their groups.

In the democratic classroom, there is a deliberate component of social action, a social agenda to improve and change classroom life. This is achieved through classroom activities that reveal social inequalities and encourage student participation in the design of alternatives. Students critique, engage in dialogue, and confront social issues.

Social Action, Student Voice, and Writing Workshop

Judging from the passion and tempest that characterized our class discussions, we expected to see some of these issues captured in student writings. A democratic classroom and writing workshop share many of the same assumptions. Both promote choice, respect for individual differences, problem solving and community. In both, the curricula are student driven and the teacher's primary role is that of facilitator.

Once we were feeling successful with class meetings as a way to build the democratic classroom, we decided to begin writing workshop. To our dismay, social action through student voice did not carry over into student writing. Instead, what they wrote about were things they thought would make good stories. They drew their inspiration from a shared culture, not the one cultivated in the classroom community, but the one they shared as nine- and ten-year-olds in Cerritos: the culture of Nintendo, X-men and the Baby-sitters Club. These were the story topics of choice.

Student peers wrote comments like "good story" on the peer conference sheets. We, on the other hand, found the stories flat and lifeless. They didn't contain any hint of the writer and the writer's life. Stories entitled "Hello Kitty," "Killer Whales," and "Trolls" figured prominently in our workshop. We felt they lacked depth and were not what we expected or hoped for. The writers seemed happy enough with the results, and their friends didn't seem to care much one way or the other. To us, however, the workshop seemed "dead" when we had hoped it would be more active and alive.

Why didn't our students write about what we considered burning issues? Why, to us, did they seem so passive? Why didn't they ask questions, write about their experiences, their classroom life? The voices we heard in class meetings were not being carried over into their writing. Class meetings worked as a venue for authentic voice and building a democratic community. Why hadn't writing workshop done the same?

We wondered what we were not seeing. Was there a cultural component to this? Ours was a predominantly Asian American classroom. As Susanne knew from personal experience, embedded in some of the Asian cultures represented in the room were strong philosophical or religious underpinnings that promoted unquestioned acceptance of the world. This meant to not question authority, particularly your teacher.

We also began to wonder if there were other forces that influenced this behavior beyond culture. What conditions made up our students' past experiences in school? Could their previous few years of schooling, however brief, have played a significant part in what appeared to be their passivity? As Sizer (1983) asserts, "Docility is not only encouraged but frequently demanded. . . . The tragedy is that the great majority of students do not rebel; they accept . . . virtually every aspect of school life as The Way Things Are" (p. 75). We began to wonder about a number of questions:

> Is it easier to be one of many fourth-grade voices in a class meeting than it is to be the sole voice in a piece of writing?
>
> What should the teacher's role be in guiding students to write about social issues? Whose passivity is being reflected here? Theirs or ours?
>
> How could the teacher help students see the value of their personal experiences and their worlds without taking away the ownership of the writing?
>
> Will a social agenda emerge naturally in writing or does the teacher have to do something?

Is writing about issues more risky because it's more personal?

Is this observed passivity in writing something that happens because of the way schools are organized?

Is the writing workshop an appropriate place for raising social and personal issues?

In keeping with our concept of the democratic classroom, we went to the students for answers to our questions. Answers ranged from "We already know about ourselves. It's boring to write about things you already know" to "We don't write about ourselves because no one cares about us."

BINGO! This last comment sparked a line of inquiry by Brenda.

BRENDA: What do you mean, no one cares about you?

STUDENTS: Adults never listen to us. They don't want to hear our stories.

BRENDA: Moi? Me? Which adults?

STUDENTS: All adults—our parents, too.
They control everything.
It takes five of us to equal one of you.
They never give us what we want.

SUZANNE: What do you want from them?

STUDENTS: Everything!

SUZANNE: Not even Santa gives you everything.

STUDENTS: Yeah, well, Santa can't be trusted because he's an adult too.

As much as we had thought we were developing a democratic classroom, where all voices, teachers and students, carried equal weight and value, obviously this was in our minds, not the students. Their feelings of equality in the classroom had to be constructed over time, through multiple experiences, forms, and interactions.

This year, working with a new group of students, we have continued the class meetings, but have rethought the writing workshop. Instead of having writing workshop, we introduced writers' notebooks (Calkins 1991) to help students document slices of life. They fill their notebooks with fascinating entries, some in Chinese or Arabic. The students are now writing about their lives, frustrations, and feelings about equity. It appears that keeping a writer's notebook has opened up the students' writing in ways we had been seeking.

Students bring their notebooks to class meetings and take notes. We have found, for example, that it is through their notebooks that the girls are able to express their feelings about the boys dominating the class discussions (Figure 8–1).

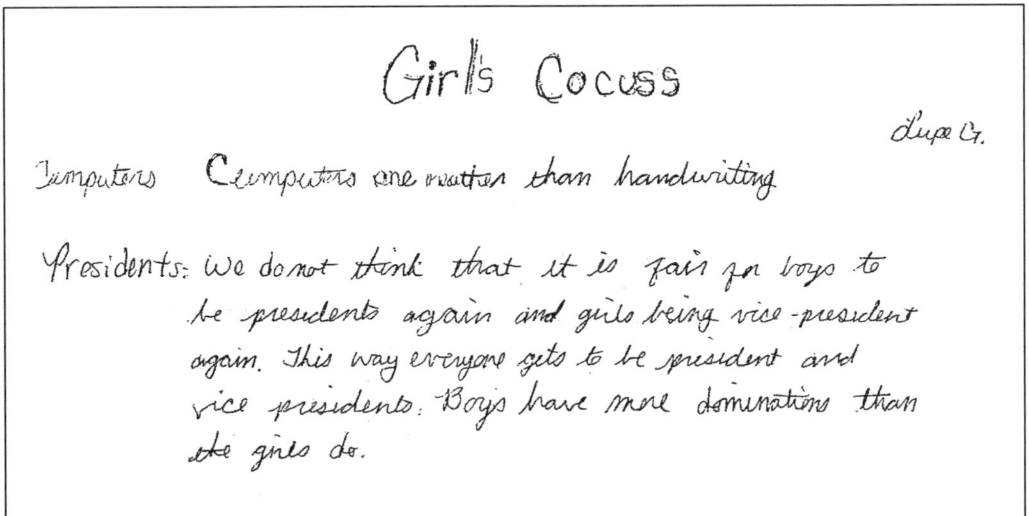

Girls Cocuss

Lupe G.

Computers   Computers one matter than handwriting

Presidents: We do not think that it is fair for boys to be presidents again and girls being vice-president again. This way everyone gets to be president and vice presidents. Boys have more domination than the girls do.

Girls Cocuss

Boys dominate girls
Girls should say when it is our turn to talk.
When we are not with Mrs. Brown or in the class, we should say something to stand up for each other.
If things don't work good, tell Mrs. Brown and she could give them a fine.

Figure 8–1 Excerpt from Lupe's Notebook

We purposefully decided to develop the sense of power the students were building. We read entries from our own notebooks that included our personal and cultural inventories and life experiences. Following is an excerpt from Suzanne's notebook:

In my family, new immigrants from China are customarily referred to as "cousins" even if they are not related to you. I admit I am not totally comfortable with most of my cousins. One reason is that their first question to me is typically, "Do you speak Chinese?" My reply is, "I listen to it, I don't speak it." My mother-in-law's English is a little choppy and I understand her. I can understand my mom who swears at the cooks at her restaurant in Chinese. (She thinks her cussing doesn't count as poor role modeling if I can't understand the language.) But there is more than just a language barrier between me and new immigrants. They make me feel guilty for dropping out of Chinese School. "Well, you would speak Chinese if your mother hadn't married an Anglo, wouldn't you?" or "It's too bad you have lost your language, have you lost the culture too?" It is as if I am impersonating a Chinese.

They referred to me as a victim of circumstance, as a lost Chinese soul in a western world. They extend their sympathies. I could never tell them I really wish I could speak in Spanish.

I'm beginning to understand the different forms of being Chinese. From the perspective of those people from China, I am not really Chinese because I've lost the language. For others, my face is Asian and I am bicultural. For me personally, I am often a cultural schizophrenic; I am an outsider and an insider in two different cultural groups.

Students responded in kind by telling us their stories of age and size discrimination, incidents of powerlessness at home and on the playground. Figure 8–2 is one such piece.

We have come to realize that building a democratic classroom takes time, thoughtfulness, and reflection on the part of both teacher and students. Our goal is to provide even more opportunities for students to engage in meaningful dialogue about their lives and the way they experience the classroom, the school, the community, and the world.

Chris Lee

"Cant We all just Get Along"

Did you ever think about you're life, what you are, what your reiligon is? I have! I'm Butes Somtimes. I feel I want a diffrent reiligon because all my other friends talk about their reiligon and Christain but, I have nothing to say about mine. No one that I know at school is butes.

Sometimes I think about my race and what I am However I wish I was some other race because some people make fun of me. I feel that I am not important, to anyone but, my self

I live in Cerritos were there are mixed reiligon race all over the place

My life is fine but one thing is in my away. The thing is what I am.

THE END

Figure 8–2
Student's
Cultural
Inventory

WENDY J. HOOD

"Did They Know He Had Slaves When They Elected Him?" Young Children Can Ask Powerful Questions

"WAIT," SAID JIM. "WAIT, WAIT. GO BACK TO THAT OTHER page." The class of thirty third graders became quiet. "They elected a president who had slaves?" I'd been reading a passage from Julius Lester's *To Be a Slave* (1968). Jim's question interrupted the reading. After a pause he went on. "Did they know he had slaves when they elected him?" I marveled at the question—and from an eight-year-old boy! I marveled at the discussion that followed it. I marveled at the depth of thinking my young students had achieved.

In the months that followed, I discussed my experience with friends and colleagues, who helped me think through what the students and I had done that had led us to be able to have such complex discussions in grade 3.

It is important to note that my students are typical third graders. They attend public school in Tucson, Arizona, and come from a variety of ethnic and socioeconomic backgrounds. About two thirds qualify for free or reduced lunch. Around half are Hispanic, three are Native American, one is African American, and the rest, as we say in the Southwest, are Anglo. The only unusual thing perhaps is that many of these students had also been with me for second grade.

The Study of Native Americans

Around the sixth week of third grade, my student teacher, Elizabeth, and I led our students into a study of Native Americans. Elizabeth began with a web of what the students already knew. Their background was highly varied. Some children knew some facts, while others repeated stereotypes such as "Indians live in teepees." We decided that in our course of study we'd need to help students come to understandings that would not only help them move beyond stereotypes but begin to recognize them as such. We also discovered a need to help students come to know that there is both a past *and a present* for most Native American peoples. After we spent a number of days exploring a variety of activities designed to meet these goals, each child self-selected one area for more in-depth study.

I thought this was working, until one day when I asked Julie what she was studying. "Indians." "What about them?" "Just Indians." Hmm . . . What to do?

Elizabeth and I decided that the kids needed a bit more direction. We decided that it would be a good idea to have them select different Native American peoples to study. The kids liked that idea. Working with the whole class, we asked the kids to brainstorm what they'd like to know. They came up with such questions as "What did they wear?" "Where did they live?" and more. We pushed them a bit. "How about finding out where they live now, too?" When one child asked if Native Americans celebrate Halloween (can you tell that it was October?) and Cherokee Eli responded, "I do," the kids themselves broadened the question to "What holidays do they celebrate?" We had the students pair off, and each pair selected a different people to study. We put together a study guide for the kids that reflected their questions.

The intensity of the study that followed took us by surprise. The students became involved in both their own and their peers' projects. Occasionally they'd discover a book that they thought all the kids should hear. Then we'd read it to the whole class. This happened with a picture book about the Trail of Tears that Eli, who was studying about his own people, had discovered. It was early November, and Bill Clinton had just been elected. We'd participated in the national Kid Voting, so the class was aware of presidential election issues. As we read the book, they immediately recognized many similarities between George Bush's campaign promises and ones made by Andrew Johnson in his reelection campaign. That was probably the first day that Elizabeth and I began to see the depth of the students' thinking.

Yet we also discovered gaps in their knowledge base. Another story we shared with the class was a picture book called *Dancing with the Indians* by Medearis (1991). It is the story of a little African American girl who attends a Seminole pow-wow. She recalls the time that her ancestor, a runaway slave, was taken in and made blood brother by the Seminole. Student response to that book was flat. They liked the poetry and the pictures but missed the impact. In a discussion following the reading, I asked why he might have run away. They thought he was running *from* the blood brothers. I think they associated the term with contemporary gangs. None could recall where the slave had run from. We reread the passage that explained that he was a slave who ran from the plantation. Still no connection was made. I finally asked, "Do you know what a slave is?" No response. Not even from the African American student. One child finally ventured, "Doesn't the Queen in England have slaves?" I explained that she probably was thinking of servants. I made a mental note to come back to the subject of slavery later on. Clearly, there was much they hadn't been exposed to.

In the end, probably nine weeks after we'd begun our study, we were pulling things together and felt done. Through their investigations and the sharing of their information, our students learned far more than what we'd expected. Stereotypes were broken. Julie, who originally thought all she had to do was study "Indians," had worked with Vicky. They reported, "The name of the Native people who live in the far north is Inuit. Sometimes they are called Eskimos, but this name is not right for Inuit people. There are many different groups of Inuit people. . . . Many people think that igloos are made of just snow, but they're not. In Inuit language igloo means shelter, so all houses and buildings are called igloos. . . . "

Images of Native Americans stuck in the past were broken. Bradley and David wrote, "Seminole girls used to help their moms cook and sew clothes. Seminole boys helped their dads hunt and fish. Now Seminole kids live near Walt Disneyworld. Maybe some even live close enough to walk there. We think they must go there a lot." Perhaps the most powerful result of our study was the opportunity it gave our Native American students to learn about themselves and to discover the bridges between past and present. Eli's report of the Cherokee included the following: "Their traditional clothes were made of deer skin and are called breechcloths. Now they wear pants, shirts, and jackets from the store. When they have celebrations they make a pipe out of little, and other sized, branches. They have pow-wows. They dance, sometimes around a fire. They dance to celebrate Say No to Drugs, prayers, and to pray to the eagle. They tell stories about the fight between the white people and the Native Americans. They also tell legends about the chief that was a chief in the past. An old man plays the drums.

"They didn't have money to buy stuff, but they had their own ways of surviving. They could get their own food and houses by hunting and making them.

"The Cherokee are one of the most creative people in the world."

Student Direction, Student Need

We knew we'd come a long way. But it still bothered me that the kids didn't know about slaves. It seemed to me a need the students had: to learn about that part of our country's past. I had always believed strongly in following the students' lead whenever possible to determine study topics. My students were used to that. I had also always begun with brainstorming what we know about a subject before beginning any study. In this case, however, I feared that the "know" session would turn up far more stereotypes than our Native American session did. I pondered how to begin.

Once I reconciled myself with my decision to teach African American history regardless of student interest, it freed me. Decisions became easier. Could I establish an atmosphere in which the kids' interest would be piqued, leading them to want to know more? Yes, I felt I could. I was concerned, however, that I knew too little about the topic myself. A product of the Detroit public schools in the 1960s, I'd learned about Eli Whitney, George Washington Carver, and Frederick Douglas for just one week every February. An occasional teacher mentioned Harriet Tubman. That was all I could recall when I assessed my own knowledge.

I began with research. The more I researched, the more I realized I knew. Oh, yes, I'd forgotten the civil rights movement! Oh, and spirituals, and civil rights songs, and jazz! The more I researched, the more I realized the kids could discover. The rich, highly developed African cultures that predate the founding of the United States, African contributions to art and math . . .

I began by establishing the environment. I got displays from our district resource center. I gathered books from every source I could find. I set all this up so that the change would greet the kids when they returned from winter break in January.

I also set up eight learning centers. I would divide the kids into small groups; each group would do one center a day over eight school days. The eight centers would vary between intense reading/writing experiences and other curricular areas. I made a center study guide for each child, with a response sheet or data collection sheet for each center. The eight centers included the following:

1. History from books. This center had the few children's
    books I could find near third-grade level. It included Milton
    Meltzer's *All times, all peoples: a world history of slavery* (1980)
    and *Now is your time: the African American struggle for Free-
    dom* by Walter Dean Myers (1991). The center guide page for
    that group had five questions: What is slavery? How did
    slaves first get to the United States? When did they first
    come? What happened when they got here? What do you
    think about what you have learned?

2. African art. This center had a number of books as well as
    some artifacts of African art. The children were invited to
    study these a while, select a style, and create an original
    work. They had a variety of media to choose from.

3. Using a textbook. Our third-grade textbook had a chapter
    on slavery and the Civil War. The students were to read
    that chapter. Again I wrote guiding questions: What was
    the Civil War? Why was it important? The students were
    also encouraged to compare the information from the
    text to information gathered from trade books about
    slavery.

4. Play an African game. In this center, the kids learned to
    play a version of an ancient African game. The game uses a
    wooden board with hollows and stones. A commercial ver-
    sion uses marbles. It is a strategy game, so the kids were
    asked to play once, write about the strategy they used,
    revise their strategy, and play again.

5. Learning about African Americans. This center had a collec-
    tion of biographies, contemporary and historical. The kids
    were to choose one and read it. The center guide asked
    them to describe why they chose that person and what they
    found interesting. It also asked why they thought that per-
    son became famous.

6. Mapping Africa. This center had the children identify the
    many countries of Africa on a map and label them on their
    own in their center guide.

7. Listening. This center had an audiotape called "I'm Gonna
    Let It Shine" (Harley 1990). The tape includes American
    civil rights songs, African American spirituals, and contem-
    porary songs of freedom from South Africa. At this center I
    asked the kids to identify a favorite song, quote the lyrics
    that appealed to them, and explain why they liked it.

8.   Learning about Martin Luther King, Jr. This center had a
     collection of biographies about Dr. King. The center guide
     had four questions: Who was Martin Luther King? Why
     was he important? What did he believe? What does this
     mean to you?

The Start of the African American Study

The morning the kids returned from winter break, the first
book I read to them was *Ashanti to Zulu* (Musgrove 1976).
They immediately saw the parallel between the varied
African peoples and the many Native American peoples
they'd studied. I introduced the centers and was pleased
and relieved by the kids' enthusiasm as they did them. Most
centers ran independently, although the history center often needed an adult to help the students find the key pages to
focus on.

I was often surprised during our center time. I found kids
reading two and three biographies about Dr. King cover to
cover and comparing the similarities. I heard kids wandering
around the room humming "Oh, Freedom." I saw kids bemoan-
ing the fact that the social studies textbook must think they're
stupid. It gave them so little information!

More began happening. When Elizabeth dropped by at
the end of the first day, Kendra, our one African American
student, greeted her with "We're studying about me now!"
The next day Kendra asked me if she could read me a
story she'd written at home the night before. It was a three-
page report about Rosa Parks. Kendra had gone home and
had told her family about our study. They told her about Rosa
Parks and the Montgomery bus boycott. She'd written it down.
I asked Kendra to read her story to the class. The kids in the
class were proud of Kendra. They wanted her to read it to all
the other classes. I suggested that maybe our class could organize an assembly for the school. After all, this year, 1993, was
going to see the first Martin Luther King state holiday in Arizona. Yes, they wanted to do that! We invited other classes to
participate. Kendra rewrote and revised her report and reread it

to the class the third day. I decided to teach the class a song I'd learned in my youth, "The Ballad of Momma Rosa Parks" (Venet and Mize 1963). To my surprise, they loved it. It became a favorite song.

The kids also began to initiate other related learning. Collette brought in a book that was over a hundred years old. It was a first printing of the writings of a freed slave. We read parts of it.

Jim was the first to notice that one book said that slaves were first brought to North America in 1609 by the Portuguese, while another cited 1492 as the date because Columbus had African slaves on his ships. Jim initiated a search of all the books we had in the center and made a chart comparing the different dates cited as the point when the first African slaves were brought to North America.

Mark brought in a newspaper clipping about a report of slavery going on in the world today and the number of countries in which children are captured or sold into slavery. I read it to the class and we discussed it. The kids easily referred to their maps as various countries were mentioned. Mark made a map he titled "Slavery in the World Today."

The students decided that the textbook was insufficient so they sought their own sources. Anna brought in a Time-Life video from the public library about the Civil War. This video quoted Lincoln as saying that his goal was to save the Union, not to abolish slavery, that if he could save the Union without stopping slavery he'd do that. They had me replay that part about five times so they could all be sure he'd really said that. (It was something I had never learned myself.)

By the time our eight days in the centers had passed, I had no doubt the students would want to continue with the topic. Their interest certainly had been aroused. When I read the kids' responses to their learning about Martin Luther King, Jr., their writing brought me to tears, it was so powerful. I took one statement from each students' writing, wrote each on an index card, and put them in logical order. Then I wrote the statements out on a piece of paper. I took that to school the next day and told the kids I had a very special poem to read to them. By the time I was done most had recognized some of the words. I told them they'd written the poem. In our assembly, each student came to the microphone one by one, in turn, to read his or her own words.

Martin Luther King was a man of peace.
He was a minister like his father.
He believed that life was not by the color of the skin but by the content of the character.
Martin Luther King is important because he made speeches and taught us to learn about others.
Martin Luther King was a good man.
Martin Luther King was a Black leader.
Martin Luther King was a Black preacher. He believed people should have their rights.
Martin Luther King was a teacher. He was a very important man.
He thought Black people had a right to do everything White people do.
Martin Luther King believed that people could do anything they want. So could kids.
Martin Luther King tried to stop something that was not fair.
Martin Luther King was a very special man. He believed that Blacks and Whites should not be separated.
Martin Luther King believed anyone could sit in the front of the bus.
Martin Luther King believed Whites are no different from Blacks so he tried to change it.
Martin Luther King believed Black people and White people should have the same laws.
Martin Luther King changed laws.
Martin Luther King was a Freedom Fighter.
Martin Luther King would fight for his rights.
Martin Luther King was a fighter. He fought people who used guns and bombs. He fought with words and ideas.
Martin Luther King was given the Nobel Peace Prize.
Martin Luther King believed everyone should get treated equally.
Martin Luther King tried to make the world a better place.
Martin Luther King brought love to everyone.
Martin Luther King believed in courage and strength.
Martin Luther King believed in equality and Justice.
He changed the world when he told his ideas out to everyone.

Individual Topics

Only after we'd completed our centers and after I'd read a number of books about African American history, including daily readings from *To Be a Slave*, did we brainstorm about what we knew and what questions we still had. Then the students chose individual topics of study. The topics were highly varied: cotton, plantations, slavery, famous slaves, Civil War, and school desegregation. They were allowed to work individually or in teams. Each individual or team came up with specific questions for their topic.

We found our school library sadly lacking in useful material, so the kids sought outside sources. They brought in encyclopedias from home and books from the public library. Some kids got their parents to take them to our city's main library for the first time. One visited the university library. One student brought me a rather curt note from the children's librarian at the local public library informing me not to make mass assignments in areas with so little resources for children. In spite of the lack of resources, we did find information. Fortunately, I was able to recruit some extra adult volunteers to help students with some of the reading of the more difficult books.

Perhaps the pair who had the most difficulty were Kendra and Stella. They wanted to learn about school desegregation. They'd seen a movie on TV about Ernest Green and an early school desegregation case and became fascinated by that topic. Unfortunately, there was nothing in any of the books in our class about desegregation. There was a bit about segregation, Jim Crow laws and such. That was a start; but these two girls, one African American, one blond-haired, blue-eyed Anglo, wanted to learn about *de*segregation. We went to our school library only to learn that it had no encyclopedias with copyright dates after court desegregation went into effect. "Desegregation" was not in any encyclopedia index. That night I got a phone call from Stella's mom. She was angry. She wanted to know why I'd assign such a tough topic to her little girl. She said, "There are no books about it at either of the two closest public libraries. We talked to the librarians, and they can't think of any they know of anywhere. And besides, segregation is a touchy subject. It was just an awful time. When I grew up in Alabama . . . " I don't remember quite what she said after that because of what I'd begun thinking. Kendra's family also had a history in Alabama. That's why Rosa Parks was so important to her family. I assured Stella's mom that the topic was Stella's choice and said that since she'd lived through it perhaps she'd take the time to talk with Stella about it. She asked if that was really okay, that Stella would just get her information from her mom and not a book. I assured her that would be great, and suggested that perhaps that was why Stella had chosen the topic in the first place, because she knew a bit about her mother's history and wanted to know more. With that reassurance, we were off.

The learning continued and the intensity mounted. A university student from Ghana visited our classroom. The children had incredible questions to ask her. "Were any of your relatives captured as slaves?" She brought powerful connections to the class. It is the visitor's people who tell the Anansi stories we'd read about. She brought a Ghanian version of the game we'd been playing and taught us that variation. She showed us a Kente like the one we'd read about in *The Black Snowman* (Mendez 1989). She told us a folktale of her people that was remarkably like *The Talking Eggs* (San Souci 1989). I was amazed at how much all the kids had learned. Then Jaime asked, "Are you a slave?" with all seriousness. Her response was wonderful. "Your grandmother's grandmother's grandmother is not alive today. Neither is mine. That was from the time of the slaves. Not now. My people were taken as slaves in that time. I was not born then. I am from Africa today. Kendra is not from Africa. Her grandmother's grandmother's grandmother is from Africa." "Oh," was all that Jaime said. But the understanding in her tone and expression spoke volumes.

During Love of Reading Week in February our school sponsored a door decorating contest. Each door was to resemble or illustrate that class's favorite book. Our class voted for *To Be a Slave* as its book. While other classes had dragons and Strega Nona on their doors, my kids were drawing pictures of slaves—naked, chained together, being lashed by whips, crammed into ships, on the auction block. One picture had a slave master speaking rudely to a slave. I was concerned, to say the least, about the pictures being displayed in the hallway. I raised my concerns to the group. They insisted that since they'd drawn the truth, ugly as it was, it should go up. Other kids should know, too, they said. The students agreed, however, that the pictures needed explanations to be properly understood. So they wrote captions such as, "Masters called slaves bad names to make them feel like animals" and "Slaves were given hardly any clothes to wear, not even *chonis* (underwear)." We didn't win the prize for the prettiest door but children and adults alike took the time to read our messages.

One day in early March, the kids came back in from lunch very upset. "Mrs. Hood, there was a kid out on the playground using stereotypes with Kendra. She called her that N word. The one we talked about. The one from *To Be a Slave*." These kids could no longer say the word "nigger" out loud. "What did you do?" I asked. "Well, we just figured she was ignorant, so we told her that word is a stereotype word and that Kendra is our friend. Then we told her how that word came from the slave owners and the Portuguese who brought the slaves here and how it was a really, really bad word and that now that she knows what it means she shouldn't use it anymore." I asked the kids if they wanted me to do anything about it. They said no, they thought they'd handled it, but that if she said it again, now that she knows what it means, I should see that she gets in big trouble!

As our work continued, we entered our research into computers in the school computer lab. We'd begun doing this the first week of January, and now, early in April, we were almost done. I asked the students if they would help me write an introduction to the book we were producing that would include our research reports, our Martin Luther King poem, and our favorite songs from this study. I began by writing the first paragraph. The rest was written by the whole group, language experience style:

Dear Reader,

In October of this school year, the third graders in Room 3 were studying about Native Americans. We read a book called *Dancing with the Indians*. It was about a slave in Florida who escaped and ran away. The Seminole people made him their blood brother. When we talked about that book, Mrs. Hood learned that our whole class did not know what a slave was. We knew there were slaves, but we didn't know what they were.

In January, we began to study African American history. We studied real hard.

Mrs. Hood read a long chapter book called *To Be a Slave* by Julius Lester. In the book it told about what they said to slaves, and it told about how the people felt about being slaves, and what they did in their church, and how slavery worked. We read a book about Harriet Tubman. She was a famous slave who ran away North and helped others to freedom.

We read *Wiley and the Hairy Man; Julian Tales; The Village of Round and Square Houses; Anansi, the Spider; A Story, A Story;* and *Mother Hubbard's Cupboard*. Mrs. Hood's mother gave us a book of African American poetry called, *Pass It On*.

Collette brought in a book that was 138 years old. It was written by a freed slave.

We did centers. At the centers we wrote about African Americans. We learned about slavery. We played an old African game. We studied African art.

We sang songs of Africa and African America. We sang civil rights songs. We all really liked the song about Mama Rosa Parks.

We did research. We asked and answered questions about African Americans. We all came up with something to study about in African American history.

A teacher from the country of Ghana, in Africa, came to visit our class and share Ghanian stories, songs, dances, and games. She also told us about Ghana and the slave castles. They are really dungeons.

Kendra wrote a story about Rosa Parks. They treated her bad on the bus. They took her to jail for no reason. She sat down on the bus. She fought for justice. They organized a boycott so that everyone could be treated equally. Now everyone can sit anywhere on the bus.

We learned a little about other famous African Americans. We learned about Malcolm X, Nat Turner, Ernest Green, Martin Luther King, Jr., Diana Ross, Whitney Houston, Bill Cosby, Magic Johnson, Michael Jordan, Jesse Jackson, Michael Jackson, and James Brown. We learned about how Martin Luther King and Malcolm X said things differently. Malcolm X used guns and knives. Martin Luther King used words, dreams, and feelings.

We organized an assembly for the whole school for Martin Luther King's birthday. We told the other kids about Dr. King and about Rosa Parks. We sang our favorite songs. We learned "We Shall Overcome" in sign language. Other classes also read poems and did plays.

That could have been the end. But it was not.

The next day, we were in class. I was reading a passage from *To Be a Slave* on George Washington and Thomas Jefferson. "Wait," Jim broke in. "Wait, wait. Go back to that other page." The class became quiet. "They elected a president who had slaves?" After a pause he went on. "Did they know he had slaves when they elected him?" I set the book down and asked, "What do you think?" The dialogue that followed was student run. Every student was involved. I watched, amazed. They were taking turns and really listening to each other. I wish I'd had a tape recorder on. I only remember snippets.

"They believed it was right, then."

"The slaves couldn't vote."

"Neither could women."

"The women wouldn't have voted for a man who owned slaves."

"Oh, it says that Martha Washington had slaves, too."

"Read that part again."

"Hey, remember last year with the dinosaurs?"

"This is real, not dinosaurs."

"No, that other book, the one about News about Dinosaurs. It said that scientists used to believe dinosaurs dragged their tails and now they don't. They changed what they believed."

"People change what they believe over time."

"Yeah, like Kent used to say bad things about Mexicans and now he knows they're stereotypes."

The discussion came back to me. "What do you think, Mrs. Hood?"

That could have been the end. But it was not.

As we prepared for our third quarter report cards, I interviewed each child. One question I asked was, "When you are an adult, what do you think you'll remember about our study of African American history?" Jaime replied, "I learned not all Africans are slaves." Kent remarked, "I learned that people are people." Juan responded, "I learned they made slaves work all the time and they would get beat if they stopped to catch their breath." Kendra's answer came very quickly: "I learned it's not all about Whites."

That could have been the end. But it was not.

As our study of African American history drew to a close, the kids reminded me that I had chosen that topic (I thought they'd forgotten), and they reminded me that I'd promised that they could select the next topic. (Maybe I had!) I was exhausted from the intensity with which we'd been working. I was hoping for a nice, light subject, or maybe a science topic, like the rain forest—something with lots of books for third graders. I tried to plant the seed by leaving them some "rain forest activities" while I was away at a conference for a couple of days. It didn't work. We brainstormed ideas, voted, and narrowed the list down. The rain forest was out on the first cut. On the final vote, the kids had elected to study Ancient Egypt. "Why?" I asked them. I hadn't made the connection they had. I thought they'd be thinking of the glory of the pharaohs. No. Slaves. There once were slaves in the land of Egypt.

It was April. I arranged to have a Passover seder in class. We began to gather mud for building bricks . . .

I think for these kids now, there will never be an end.

JANET NELSON

All Together Now: Engagement, Collaboration, and Problem Solving in the Multi-Age Classroom

RECENTLY, REGULAR AND SPECIAL EDUCATION TEACHERS in my school challenged themselves to move from teaching relatively homogeneous self-contained classes to coteaching more heterogeneous multidevelopmental and multi-age classes, with the express purpose of including mainstream special education students. Philosophically, it was a wonderful idea, but there was a problem. It stemmed from our changing the mix of students in the classrooms without changing what happened in those classrooms. We attempted to use established first-through third-grade curricula to teach a wide range of students. It soon became obvious that we were asking students to adapt to the demands of the curriculum. We were creating what Elkind (1989a) has called "curriculum disabled students." Instead, we needed to adapt the curriculum to the students.

This meant that we needed to find strategies that would foster holistic, relevant, meaning-centered learning (Turnure 1986; Howells 1992; Keirns 1993) and create active classrooms that would encourage students to take risks, experiment, and build knowledge by connecting what they already know with what they experience in the real world (Turnure 1986; Elkind 1989a). We needed strategies that would support learning in collaboration with others (Goldstein and Goldstein 1980; Elkind 1989b; Howells 1992). More specifically, as a special education teacher, I needed to find strategies that would enable me to provide learning opportunities that would accommodate a wide range of student ability levels (Goldstein and Goldstein 1980; Elkind 1989b).

Out of a number of teaching methods and ideas I tried in my classroom, one stood out as particularly successful. Based in part on my understanding of and experience with a teaching method called Scottish Storyline, as developed by the staff of Jordanhill College of Education in Glasgow (Fifield 1990), the children and I developed a curriculum strategy for social studies that guided their learning through collaborative problem-posing and problem-solving.

Topics of study were based on my observations of student interest or were taken from the scope and sequence of mandated curriculum. In either case, topics developed naturally in response to questions or problems posed by either the students or myself as we progressed in our exploration of the theme. Our learning evolved from answering these questions and solving the problems that we encountered along the way. The extent of a student's participation in generating questions and posing and solving problems was determined by developmental level. Everyone was included, and because it could be made appropriate to everyone's developmental level, previous behavior management problems decreased dramatically. Learning was assessed through learning logs and multimedia portfolios of work.

The following are two examples of primary social studies topics explored through our problem-posing and -solving approach.

The Restaurant

Our first topic developed from student interest. Although it took place in my special education classroom of six- to eight-year-olds (with developmental ages from two to five), it is applicable to a wide range of students.

After taking a field trip to a local restaurant and being treated to pie as part of their study of communities, our students began playing restaurant with toys from the free choice box. Their activity centered around piling up plastic food on cafeteria trays, shoving the trays in the faces of unsuspecting classmates, and yelling, "Here's your food!"

From this I could tell they were interested in restaurants and that they knew restaurants had to do with distributing food. It could have been that they liked the attention they got playing the adult role of waiter, or maybe it was the apple pie and strawberry tarts piled three inches high with whipped cream.

In either case, this became their topic, and The Restaurant took on a life of its own as the students made new connections between what they already knew and what they were experiencing. It also points out the power of ownership in learning, the structure of the questioning process, and the role of the teacher and students as collaborators.

The study begins as teacher and students create a setting and roles for themselves to play as they explore the theme topic.

Developing the Setting

Perhaps the best way to show the relation between questions we asked, activities we performed, and the learning that resulted is to present the three in tabular form.

Students kept a learning log of their own ideas in pictures, dictation to the teacher, or their own text after each activity.

Questions	Activities	Learning Outcomes
Where will our restaurant be?	Students suggested practical and impractical locations: classroom, cafeteria, school library.	Concept of location in relation to landmarks in a classroom and school. Language of position.
How will people know it's there?	We discussed ways we tell, visually and verbally, where our classroom, our school, a store, or a fast food restaurant is located: "Our number on the door," "TV," neon signs, written signs, numbers.	Idea of conveying important information through spoken and printed language.
	(I tried to convince students not to hold a popularity contest to choose the "best" anything. Rather, we should reach decisions democratically. We chose to make a sign.)	Experiencing democratic process.
What should our sign say?	We made a list of popular restaurants.	Working cooperatively with classmates to produce a product.
Should we use someone else's restaurant name or do we want our own?	(To my disappointment, students stuck with a compilation of names of national restaurants.)	
	Students decided to use "smelly" markers for the sheer pleasure of it and then switched to fluorescent markers.	Locating and acquiring resources for sign making.
How will we make the sign? What will we need to make it? Where can we get those things?	Having answered these questions, students worked cooperatively to make signs.	Using prior knowledge to solve a new problem. Using language of description. Measuring. Drafting.

Questions	Activities	Learning Outcomes
What will our restaurant look like?	We talked about what restaurants we have visited look like. (Because my students were more interested in acting out the restaurant than in decorating it, they chose to start with our box of plastic food, playdough, a couple of cafeteria trays, and chairs.) Depending on developmental level, students could do anything from setting up a play restaurant with real accoutrements to designing architectural blueprints for their own hypothetical restaurant.	Designing and constructing models individually or cooperatively.

DEVELOPING ROLES

Next, we worked out who the participants were in a restaurant setting, and what they did.

Questions	Activities	Learning Outcomes
Who will come to the restaurant?	Students came up with a list including people, classmates, friends, the principal, the P.E. teacher, favorite cartoon characters, and stuffed animals. My developmentally younger students wanted to come to the restaurant as themselves, because they weren't ready to identify with a character outside of themselves. More developmentally advanced students may be able to identify with their roles as a doll, puppet, mask, or figure in a mural and may write a biography for the customer, including favorite kinds of food.	Locating and acquiring resources to make dolls, puppets, masks, etc. May involve group written communication.
How will they know we have a restaurant here?	The students debated the relative merits of "Please come over" versus "Get down here!" They decided we should ask in a friendly way, and tell people where the restaurant is in words or pictures (i.e., a map).	

Questions	Activities	Learning Outcomes
How do stores and restaurants get us to come? (This from me.)	Students responded, "They tell us to come." One student sang a well-known advertising jingle that ended with, "It's your kind of store!" We then wrote the words to the song on chart paper and analyzed them as a written advertisement. When we analyzed advertisements from newspapers and magazines, even students who don't read noticed the bright colors and stand-out print. More advanced students determined a need for a symbol or logo to stand for the restaurant and designed one. Students might also work cooperatively to make their own print or television ad using the same questions they asked in making the sign.	Idea that polite words convey friendliness and may be more inviting. Converting spoken words to printed text. Using position words to convey directions. Drawing and following a map to a specific location. Concept that simple symbols, combinations of letters, and pictures called logos can be used to stand for big ideas.
Why will they want to come to our restaurant? Why do we go to restaurants? (My question.)	Students responded, "To get Happy Meals, to get Blizzards." I helped them summarize. "We go to restaurants to eat, right? To eat foods we like." We dictated a list of foods we like to eat when we go to a restaurant.	Recall real life experience from memory.
How will people get food in our restaurant? Who will bring them the food?	Role-play ways we get food in restaurants: drive through, cafeteria, buffet, table service. After some discussion, students chose table service, because they all wanted to play waiter, although drive-through was a strong second because they all wanted to drive the car.	Idea that different means can be used to reach the same goal.

SOLVING PROBLEMS

The next step includes the ways the students in their roles interact with each other, and the events and problems that they encounter. Generally speaking, the more abstract the topic, in concept, time, or place, the more the teacher has to orchestrate incidents from historical information and has to suggest key questions in order to promote topic development. Concrete real life topics, like our restaurant, tend to generate questions and problems on their own.

Our advertising had been successful, people (real ones) from our classroom and school did arrive at our restaurant, and they wanted to eat. True to their free play experience, waiters were still piling food on cafeteria trays, which they pushed on unsuspecting customers. The customers were pushing it right back with, "I don't want this! Don't give it to me!" Thus, we were provided with our first problem.

Questions	Activities	Learning Outcomes
How can the customers get the food *they* want?	Students suggested that the customers either get the food out of the box themselves or make their own food. Students eventually rejected these ideas because they took away the fun of being a waiter ("But then the waiter doesn't get to do anything"). Students said, "Tell the waiter to get the food for us."	Cooperative problem-solving skills.
How will the waiter remember what each customer wants?	Students said, "If the waiter forgets, go ask the customer, again and *again*." The student customers eventually got tired of this and started complaining. The group then generated new suggestions: draw a picture of it; write it down yourself (waiter); ask the customer to write it.	
Who actually makes the food in the restaurant? (I role played the waiter in an actual incident, and said, "Mia wants pizza, but it's not *my* job to make pizza." Who will make the pizza?	Answering this key question resulted in an extended group question-and-answer process.	

The students truly did not seem to know where the food came from, so I asked a frequent hot lunch patron, "Brooke, are you going to eat hot lunch in the cafeteria today?"

"Yes."

"Are *you* going to make the lunch?"

"No."

"Who, what person, *is* going to make your lunch?"

"I don't know."

We tried a different point of reference. "Brooke, where are you going to eat lunch?"

"In the cafeteria."

"Who makes the food in the cafeteria?"

"The girls at the window give it to us."

"Maybe the girls make the food in the cafeteria?"

"Maybe. I don't know."

It was actually lunchtime, so we made a trip to the lunchroom. "Let's look around carefully and see if we can tell where the food is coming from."

"Brooke, you're having hot lunch today."

"No, I'm having salad bar."

"Okay, then let's look closely at who's making the salad."

"Mr. Jones?" (The lunchroom custodian.)

"Mr. Jones helps us clean up the lunchroom. Let's see who's making the salad." Students notice (thankfully) that Mrs. Smith, the school cook, is chopping carrots and carrying them to the carrot bowl on the salad bar.

"Mrs. Smith! Mrs. Smith is doing the salad bar."

"*Yes!* Mrs. Smith does the job of making food! Let's ask her what we call her job."

Once armed with this new knowledge, a student volunteered to be the cook for our restaurant. At advancing developmental levels, students might be interested in writing a job description and interviewing for the job.

The development of our restaurant continued.

Questions	Activities	Learning Outcomes
How will the cook know what food the customer wants?	The students responded, "We could show them on the paper. The waiter could draw it or write it down and show the cook."	Learning the function of writing and rereading as a memory cue.

Questions	Activities	Learning Outcomes
What can the cook do if we don't have the food?	Students suggested, "We can make food out of playdough, or we can tell the customer we don't have any." This, however, led to upset customers. I suggested asking the customers if they would like something else. Students decided they could tell the customer, "The restaurant is out of that food, would you like something else?" With the delays, the customers were getting hungry and restless as they waited for their food.	Using socially acceptable language to get needs met.
What can we give the customers to make them less hungry and keep them happy as they wait?	Students suggested bringing them candy, gum, chips, or something to drink. (This last idea won out because we really did have water.)	
How can we give them water?	Waiters went to look for cups for water. (Ditto for cutlery—everyone was eating with their fingers.) The customers didn't want to share cups and to drink other people's germs.	Concept of hygiene.
How can we get rid of the germs?	Waiters rushed to wash cups. Eventually, feeling overwhelmed, they urged customers to wash cups. (Teacher intervened to ask if that was okay with customers. It wasn't.)	Cooperation in the workplace. Verbal problem solving with real-life, concrete referents to pair with the words.
Who else can wash cups, so the waiters can do other things to help the customers?	Students volunteered to wash cups. (With waterplay in the sink, it turned out to be a very popular job.)	Concept of division of labor and job responsibilities. Sequencing actions in a job.
Who else could do that job?	More advanced students might develop a job description for cup washing and interview prospective applicants.	Filling out an application. Interviewing.

Questions	Activities	Learning Outcomes
The cook noticed that the food was running out. What will happen when all the food is given out and eaten up? How can we get more food?	Students figured out ways to replace the missing food: make it from play-dough; grow it on The Farm (a previous topic).	Idea of trading money for goods and services.
How do you get more food when you run out at your house? (My question.)	"Mom buys it." "Buy it? So, you go to the store and pay for it with money?" "Yes." "Maybe we could get more food for the restaurant from the store?" "Yes." "If we want to get some food from the store, we need to pay for it with money?" "Yes, we need to get some money for the restaurant."	Using prior knowledge to solve a new problem.

Math computation. Use of a calculator. |
| How can we get money at the restaurant? | Students reviewed what happens when you go to a restaurant. For example, "When we go to the drive-through window, Mom or Dad has to give them money before they give us food." I suggested, "Maybe our customers could give us money for the food we give them." (Although it's a stretch to remember what the money will be used for, the students like the idea of getting it.) | |
| How will they know how much money to give us? | Students remembered, "They tell you on the loudspeaker, or they write it on a note." So waiters began writing random numbers on the notepapers they gave to the cook and customers. A waiter tripped as he brought a plate heaped with all sorts of food along with the pizza Mia ordered. Mia told the waiter, "I didn't order the extra food. Please take it back." Others joined Mia in asserting themselves and began watchdogging the waiters. | Language of self-assertion. Using language to get needs met. |

Questions	Activities	Learning Outcomes
What can you tell the waiter that will fix the problem?	I asked Mia, "Is this what you wanted? Is this okay?" Mia replied, "No, I want pizza. Just pizza." Eventually, the cook became overwhelmed trying to make food we didn't have out of playdough.	
How can we help the cook?	Students dictated a list of the plastic food in the free choice box and referred to the list of favorites from a previous restaurant theme activity. They added drawings and magazine cutouts to illustrate their lists and duplicate them for distribution by the waiters. At this menu stage, students might be interested in creating a restaurant cookbook and writing and trying out their own recipes. I suggested they look at a real menu to see what they could learn. Another problem: customers were running out of money due to arbitrarily large bills issued by the waiters.	Vocabulary development. Meaning-centered writing and reading. Using language to get needs met. Writing directions. Following a sequence of steps. Measuring.
How much money should the waiters ask for?	Students added prices to the menu. They also suggested giving the customers the restaurant money or taking whatever the customers could give. Waiters were losing track of money. Coins were rolling on the floor, and paper money was blowing across the room.	Counting by 1's, 5's, 10's. Counting on and back. Making change. Using a calculator.
How can we keep track of this money?	Students suggested safe places to put the money: a box; their backpacks. These ideas made them worry about who would get to take the money home. They decided the money should stay in the classroom. Their answers then moved to possibilities such as "Give it to the teacher" or "Use the thing they put it in at the restaurant." (Eventually, I brought in a toy cash register.)	

Thanksgiving

Some topics, especially those with an historical basis, are more predictable. The Restaurant theme primarily involves "fundamental knowledge" (Elkind 1989a) that students construct for themselves by connecting their own background information with new experiences in the environment. The Thanksgiving theme, like many traditional social studies topics, is more concerned with "derivative knowledge"—knowledge constructed by others that students acquire secondhand. Because the topic of Thanksgiving is actually in the traditional second-grade social studies scope and sequence, it was comparatively easy to interest primary first- and second-grade mainstream teachers in collaborating on its development as a topic for the multi-age primary classroom with mainstream special education students. (These students had developmental levels ranging from four to nine years of age.)

When topics aren't student initiated, extra care must be taken to foster engagement and ownership. In this case, we used an emotional link, identifying with the experience of loss and dislocation, to promote engagement with the theme. Although the topic itself is a stretch for students who aren't ready to identify with characters outside of themselves (especially in another time and place), we made the activities more concrete and supportive by having students role play with real props using group dictation.

DEVELOPING ROLES

The following outlines the questions and activities the students and I used to develop the roles for the Thanksgiving study. Students maintained a portfolio of materials they produced during this study. Class videos were also made of cooperative group activities.

Questions	Activities	Learning Outcomes
Did you ever have to move away? Did you like it? How did it feel to leave the place you lived?	Students described their own experiences and drew parallels to the Pilgrims' experience: leaving home, loss of friendships, arduous travel, fear of the unknown, loneliness.	Vocabulary development. Learning to talk about feelings, negative and positive, around loss and dislocation.

DEVELOPING THE SETTING

Next, we developed the setting. Again, activities and learning followed from the questions that were asked.

Questions	Activities	Learning Outcomes
Did you want to move to a new place?	Debated the pros and cons of traveling to the New Land.	Students reflect on their own willingness to take risks.
Would you choose to go on the *Mayflower* or would you choose to stay home?	Students made models of themselves and placed them on a paper mural on a model of the *Mayflower* or on the dock.	
What do you suppose it was like on the *Mayflower*?	Students researched to the extent of their ability (including reading library books with the teacher).	Vocabulary Development. Research skills. Meaning-centered reading and writing.
	Students made their own murals of the *Mayflower* to keep in their journals. We explored the thought "If I were on the *Mayflower* . . . " and recorded responses in journals and as a class dictation.	Visual motor practice. Designing and making a model.
What do you suppose you would or would not find in the New Land?	I suggested there wouldn't be houses, McDonald's, and computer games; but there would be Native Americans, deer, wild birds, and trees. We added models of indigenous people, plants, and animals to their murals and brought in realia to experience.	Concepts about ecology and Native Americans. Idea of indigenous vs. foreign. Research skills.

Working Through the Topic
Finally, we approached the first Thanksgiving.

Questions	Activities	Learning Outcomes
What would you need to have in order to stay alive in the New Land?	Students prioritized survival needs. Students discussed ways to meet these needs.	Facts about human survival needs.
	I introduced the idea of a guide to life in the New Land named Chief Squanto. Students added Squanto, Pilgrims, shelter, food, and survival tools to their murals and role played and built models.	Concept of a guide or mentor. Linear measurement. Model design and construction.
Was Chief Squanto helpful to the Pilgrims?	Some students might be interested in researching Squanto.	
Do you let people know when you're grateful that they helped you?	Students prepared a thank-you celebration using the Native American custom of the "Corn Dance," in which popcorn is thrown into the fire (we used an air popper).	Concept of turning liquid into gas. Vocabulary development.
Would the Pilgrims like to show him they're grateful for his help? How might they do that?	As a follow-up, my students generated a list of adjectives from which they made free-verse poems describing their experience.	Describing sensory experience in words.
	I informed the students that Chief Squanto's cooperation is remembered now as Thanksgiving Day.	
Do you think *we* could cooperate and share in the way that Chief Squanto did?	We did a cooperative "jigsaw" activity in which students took turns playing Chief Squanto and giving the group directions on making simple food: popcorn, butter, cranberry juice, or toasted pumpkin seeds.	Peer teaching. Cooperation. Sequential actions to produce a product. Practice of visual motor skills.
	Students were assigned one of four food items indigenous to the New Land, with the job of trading with classmates to accumulate all four.	Vocabulary development. Language of diplomacy and cooperation. Benefits of trading and sharing.

With this approach, our multi-age and special education students were able to work together to relearn the lessons of Thanksgiving—resourcefulness, sharing, and cooperation—that were appropriate for them. In The Restaurant, rather than acquiring facts about a narrow range of knowledge chosen by the teacher, students gained the tools of problem solving and collaboration that will sustain them as lifelong learners in confronting problem-posing situations of their own.

DIANA MAZZUCHI

Map-Making and Neighborhood Exploration in a Multi-Age Classroom

*I*T WAS THE FIRST YEAR OF TEAM-TEACHING (SIXTY CHIL-
dren ages six through ten, first through third grades) in three
multi-age self-contained classes for me and my partners, Nancy
Brooks and Maggie Shine. In setting up the multi-age configu-
ration we conferred with our staff about expectations, thoughts,
and concerns. The fourth-grade teachers were concerned that
the children coming from our class would not have learned the
same concepts as the other third graders, particularly since Vermont Studies were required in fourth grade. The Neighborhood
was generally a mandated social studies topic for third grade to
prepare for Vermont Studies. To deal with the fourth-grade
teachers' concern, we chose "People and Neighborhoods" as
our umbrella theme for that year. As part of the theme, we
decided to familiarize our students with the school and the
neighborhood surrounding it. Mapping the area seemed like a
good way to start. We thought we'd probably spend three to
four weeks on it.

The art teacher began the study by having each class in our
multi-age group map the playground. The idea was to create
three class maps by incorporating each child's perceptions into
one map for that grade. The children went out to sketch what
they saw. Because of multi-age grouping, there was a variety of
ability to put down on paper what was seen. No one's map was
expected to be the same as anyone else's. Stephanie, age nine,
focused on the area she enjoyed playing in: the wooden construction, the swings and slides, and the baseball area she and
others frequently used for kickball (Figure 11–1). To judge from
her map, Stephanie sees the school as very long and surrounding most of the play space. She included the hardtop path that
is always kept cleared of snow in the winter so groups can go
for walks around the school. Chris, ten, a special needs student,
drew only certain things with no indication of the building
itself, other than a corner. But his pictures of the slide, swings,
and hopscotch area are very detailed (Figure 11–2). Rebekka, six
and a half, drew the many windows she passes when walking
around the school. She indicated the uneven shape of the school
building much as Stephanie did (Figure 11–3). Chris labeled
nothing, Rebekka labeled the area she is not allowed on, and
Stephanie identified the different areas of the playground. Their
maps helped us begin. We started where *they* were, not with
where a text said they should be.

We gathered some songs, poems, and books on mapping and
began building the children's knowledge and understanding

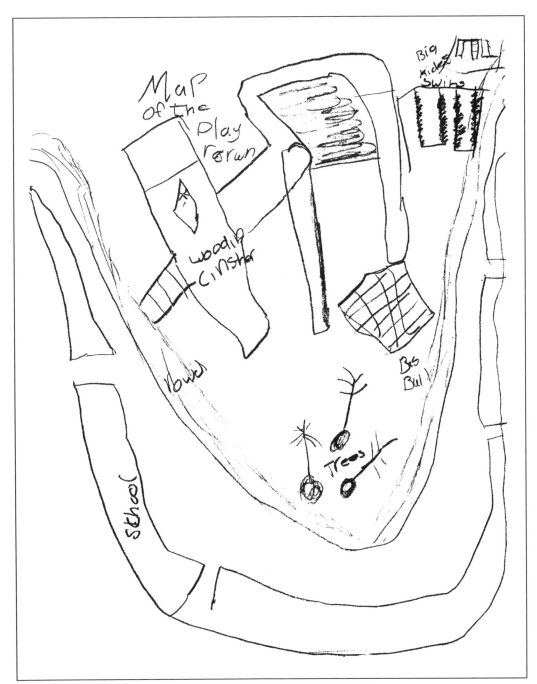

Figure 11–1 Stephanie's Map

Figure 11–2
Chris's Map

during our Shared Reading and Theme times (see schedule, Figure 11–4). Three books were particularly useful: Sally Cartwright's *What's in a Map?*, Vicki Cobb's *Sense of Direction*, and Jack Knowlton's *Maps and Globes*. We found that some of the first maps of history were made in the dirt, so the art teacher took the children outside and had them work in groups to build three-dimensional maps of the playground using sticks and other natural materials. That activity led to a discussion of ways people kept maps so they could be reused.

In the classroom during theme time we began working on our classroom maps. How accurately can we show someone

Figure 11–3 Rebekka's Map

Figure 11–4
Daily Schedule

8:30– 9:00	Opening calendar	Total group
9:00– 9:30	Shared reading	Total group
9:30– 9:45	Snack and recess	Home group
9:45–11:00	Language arts	Home group
11:00–11:40	Small-group activity time	Assigned
	Maggie: Books, science, math, listening, art	
	Nancy: Books, blocks, drama, writing, problem solving	
	Diana: Books, fine motor, games, computer, maps	
11:45–12:35	Lunch and lunch recess	
12:40– 1:10	Chapter book and sharing	Total group
1:10– 2:00	Math groups	Assigned
2:00– 2:30	Theme (science, social studies, health)	Total group
2:30– 2:50	Class meetings	Home group

else what our classroom looks like? The children devised ways to show others their classroom through a pencil-drawn map. Becky, seven, drew a map, like Chris's playground map, that showed only a few things: the pencils, markers, and crayons; the cooking materials (especially the dustpan which she frequently used); and the Grow Lab, with which she was fascinated (Figure 11–5). Chelsea, six, included a lot of detail (Figure 11–6). The outer parts of the room on her map were correctly placed. The inner parts had a few labels, but were crowded and disorganized. The tables were drawn as round when in fact they were rectangular. The cubbies were drawn with our pet parakeet on top along with our mailboxes. She understood the need to represent things but had not reached an ability to represent them with a symbol so that a map is not too crowded. Nathan, nine, stood on a chair to draw his map from a bird's-eye view (Figure 11–7). He included a key for things that in Chelsea's map were direct representations. One of the exciting things that happens in a multi-age classroom is that diversity is seen as positive. There were so many different ways that maps were made. Children got ideas from each other.

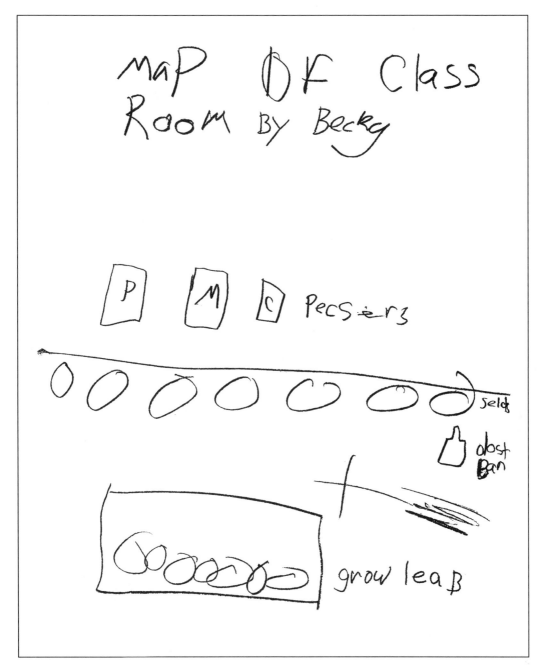

Figure 11–5 Becky's Map

Figure 11-6
Chelsea's Map

Our librarian located a video program for us called *It's a Rainbow World*. One episode, "How Do I Get There?" is the story of two children and how they find the way to Kay's party. It introduces the idea of using maps to locate places you want to go to. It shows how maps are used in work, in travel, and in locating objects. Suddenly maps of all kinds began appearing in the classroom. Katie brought in a map of Paris that had been hanging in her home for years, but that she had never paid any attention to.

Figure 11–7 Nathan's Map

We set up a map activity area in my room for all the maps we were collecting. This area was available during small-group activity time when children could choose an area to work in. One activity involved finding something hidden in the classroom by following a map to locate it. Then the children began making maps to tell where something was in the room. I found a map left on my desk telling me how to find a child's chocolate chip cookie from lunch.

The children discovered that many maps have grids. This led to discussions of how grids were used. We teachers created several activities for the map center using some of the maps children had brought in. Starting with a map of our community, children worked in multi-age groups to locate specific places such as the Creamery Bridge, the town common, and the police station by using the grid system. Then children started making question sheets ("In what square is _____?"), listing places they wanted others to locate on the town map.

We thought we could end our now eight-week study of maps with a look at our immediate school neighborhood. Our school is located in a small village on a main thoroughfare, rural route 9. We began by asking the students to list what we might see along the road. Their list included houses, several small mom-and-pop stores, and the local Brattleboro Child Development Center (BCD) across the street, which many of our students had attended. Since there was so much more—about twenty businesses and forty houses—we decided a walk might be enlightening. We spent an afternoon walking and mapping the area half a mile to the east and another afternoon mapping half a mile to the west of the school. Each child was given a clipboard, paper, and pencil. Before we left we brainstormed some symbols we could use for houses, for churches, and for businesses so that we could quickly record what we saw. As we left, we all made a large dot on our paper to show where our map would start. That dot was the only thing the maps ultimately had in common. Given the fact that our students ranged in age from six to ten years old, we expected a wide variety in their representational abilities. The actual results were fascinating.

Several decisions had to be made fairly quickly. What about where we crossed the Whetstone Brook? Should we show other streets as we crossed them? Were the fire station and the post office businesses? What about when people lived upstairs but the downstairs was a business? The children chose what and how to represent what they saw.

Many of the younger children made marks indiscriminately on the paper. Not planning ahead and running out of space, they wrote on the back. For some, that happened shortly after we left the classroom. Most of the seven-year-olds drew their maps along a more or less straight line, but they weren't particularly interested in accuracy. The older children struggled to get everything in the proper place; some tried to make sure the distance between buildings was exactly to scale. Putting the two segments of paper representing west of school and east of school together was interesting, because most did not match up.

The first thing we did after returning to the classroom was talk about what we had seen. The children were amazed at how many businesses existed on Western Avenue. It was apparent that the western end was more business-oriented than the eastern end. Where before they had identified only BCD, the church near the school, and a few stores, they now realized there were insurance offices, dentists' offices, a video and printing shop, the post office and fire station, another church, several restaurants, two apartment complexes, and many houses. We discussed the difference between businesses that supply a product, such as Martin's TV and Video, and businesses that provide a service, such as the dentist.

Groups of four or five students got together to share their maps. There was much discussion about how all the members of the group differed in their representation of what they had seen. Even the three teachers' maps differed! We decided that, within each group, members would combine their maps to create a group map.

On another day, each group was given a large piece of drawing paper. Everyone began by placing the school, with the road extending left and right, in the middle of the paper. Spreading the maps out all over the floor, we asked the children to make use of whatever they needed in the classroom to finish their maps. Tiles, unifix cubes, pattern blocks, and many other materials were put to use to represent the houses, stores, and businesses in our neighborhood. The children referred to their own and each other's maps as they created their group floor map. The custodian had a break from vacuuming our floors that evening, for there was not an inch of space left uncovered in all three classrooms.

The next day, the children began to use pieces of paper to transform the three-dimensional materials to one-dimensional ones. As they did so, we heard much discussion among the groups.

"What does Zinn Graphics do?"

"I didn't realize there was a church here."

"I never saw that building before. I wonder what it is."

The finished maps were wonderful! There had been great collaboration and cooperation, and the maps were fairly accurate. Our topic was complete—or was it?

We asked the students if they would like to find out more about the businesses they had identified in our neighborhood. We looked back at our after-walk list of all the places we had seen and put on our maps. Students formed interest groups to learn more about a particular business. Together they wrote down what they already knew about the business and what they wanted to find out. They listed questions they were curious about and they noted how they might find the answers to their questions, and how they might show what they learned (Figure 11–8).

The questions they made up were interesting. They all wanted to know how much people were paid. At the time, Vermont was going through an economic recession, and the children were hearing lots of anxious talk about money. Other questions included the following:

When did ——— get started?

What do you sell?

How many people work here?

What do you have to know how to do to work here?

Has ——— ever been somewhere else?

It became obvious to the children that the answer to the question "How will we find out?" could not be found in books. They made the decision to go directly to the source.

A member of each group made a phone call (Figure 11–9) or wrote a letter asking for permission to visit. All group members were involved in deciding what to say in the letter. In small groups children role-played interviewing. How would they interview someone in a grocery store if a customer was there? How could all members of the group be involved? What would the other group members do while one was asking a question?

When appointments had been set, parents volunteered to walk with the children and serve as official photographers. (Each parent brought a camera to take photos.) All members of

Figure 11–8
Planning Form

Group # _____ Date_____

Names _____

_____

_____

What do you know about . . . ?

_____

_____

_____

What do you want to find out about?

_____

_____

_____

Write some questions (at least 3):

_____

_____

_____

_____

How will you find out about . . . ?

_____

_____

_____

How will you show what you learned?

_____

_____

_____

_____

Figure 11–9
Guide for phone
call to set up
interview

Group # _____ Date_____

We want to visit _____

Telephone number _____

This is what you can say: "We are in the multi-age class at Academy School."

1. We are studying _____ , and _____ children would like to come visit.

2. What day of the week would be best?
   Mon.   Tues.   Wed.   Thurs.   Fri.   Sat.   Sun.

3. What time of day would be best?

   morning —
   afternoon —
   the best time —

4. This is how you can end the phone call: "Thank you. We will call you back and let you know when we will be coming."

the group went to the business and participated in the interview. Parents completed an observation sheet they returned to us after the interview (Figure 11–10). Over the course of four weeks, students visited and interviewed fourteen establishments, ranging from the Brattleboro Child Development Center (BCD) to local grocery stores, a bank, the post office, and the fire station. Other places studied were Academy School, the information booth, Whetstone Brook, and our famous covered bridge, the Creamery Bridge. Members of the brook group had their parents' permission to explore the course of the brook with an adult accompanying them.

Members of each group collaborated to writ up the information they had obtained. Final reports, which included photographs, were displayed in the hallway. Parents were invited to see the playground maps, the neighborhood maps, and the research reports. Later the reports and pictures were made into a book we called *Our Neighborhood*.

Although a social studies textbook might have been a good resource, we never felt a need to use one. Besides, in a multi-age classroom, a textbook designed for a particular grade level is

Date:	Trip to:			
Child's name				
List questions child asked				
Comments child made				
Seem focused?	yes ___ no ___	yes ___ no ___	yes ___ no ___	yes ___ no ___
Listening	yes ___ no ___	yes ___ no ___	yes ___ no ___	yes ___ no ___
Comments				

Reproduced with permission from Bridges, Goodman & Goodman 1994 *The Whole Language Catalog: Forms for Authentic Assessment* (Macmillan/McGraw-Hill, USA)

Figure 11–10
Parent Observation Sheet

hardly ever appropriate. Textbooks assume a level of information that all students have and that all are ready for. For us, the information, even the ideas for the research, came through our own exploration of the neighborhood. This exploration led from one picture of our neighborhood before the study to a much more detailed and accurate one after. Our questions led us to use "real" books on mapping and authentic activities designed in response to the students' needs. Our simple study of maps, originally planned for four weeks, turned into an integrated study that lasted sixteen weeks. When it was finished, we were confident that our students had not only the content background to cope with the fourth-grade curriculum on Vermont studies, but much more besides: they had used interviewing skills and worked cooperatively as a group. They had learned that *they* could find the answers to their questions. Now, they had a process for finding information that could be applied throughout life.

12

ROBIN CAMPBELL

Reading for Information with Young Children

THE PRACTICE OF READING STORIES ALOUD TO A PRIMARY class is well established, and for good reason. We know that children gain so much from those experiences (Teale 1984). In particular, by hearing stories read aloud, children learn about books and the organization of language. Furthermore, they learn about story structure. And, having learned about story structure, children are aided in their own reading of stories and their attempts to write them.

Of course, children try to read material other than stories, although they may not receive as much adult support for those other types of reading. Littlefair (1991), using the ideas of Halliday, categorizes children's reading into literacy, expository, procedural, and reference genres. As teachers, we need to support that variety of reading because children need to become confident with the many different texts that they will meet.

Children may find reading textbooks especially difficult. For that reason it makes sense for the teacher of young children to read information books to the class on occasion so that the vocabulary, syntactic forms, meanings, and patterns of discourse of that genre begin to become familiar.

With young children, K-2, we know that story readings often take on the form of a conversation with both teacher and children making substantial contributions to the reading (Campbell 1990). In relation to such story readings, Trelease (1989) notes that the teacher has to avoid becoming unnerved by the various comments from the children. Indeed it becomes the role of the teacher to try to read the text, make comments, use the comments from the children, and keep the reading moving forward. Reading stories to children requires skill. But what about reading expository or information books to children? It is unlikely to be any less demanding for the teacher, but it may be an especially helpful literacy activity for the children.

Let us look at the teacher with a class of six-year-old children in London, England. These grade-one children were in an "infant" (K-2) school. There were thirty children in the class; more than half of them were entitled to free school meals. In most respects, this was a typical class of lively, inquisitive children who were curious about their environment.

The class was engaged in a study of the ecological topic of rubbish: What happens to our rubbish? Where does it go? What can be recycled? The children had observed rubbish being collected, had talked about it, and had then written and drawn about those experiences. The teacher had encouraged a consideration of some historical aspects in that study: What used to happen to rubbish? Was that healthy for people? To support that part of the study a number of relevant books had been collected, and although some of those were written as stories, and were therefore in the literary genre, a number were expository.

As part of a whole-class read-aloud the teacher gathered the children on the rug to read from the book *Famous Cities: London* (Quest Books 1979). The book demonstrated how the depositing of rubbish in the streets contributed to the Great Fire of London and therefore dramatically illustrated the need for devising other ways to deal with rubbish. First, the teacher devoted time to setting the scene for the children. They were asked to recall their discussion from the previous day and by doing so they were encouraged to think about the prior knowledge that they could bring to this literacy event.

TEACHER: Well, yesterday I was talking to you about what it was like a long, long time ago in London. What were the houses made of? Who can remember?

ASHLEY: Wood.

TEACHER: Yes, they were made of wood, weren't they? And what was another thing about those houses? Not only were they made of wood, but something else.

SHAUN: They had dirty streets.

TEACHER: They had dirty streets, yes. Why did they have dirty streets?

NICKY: They didn't have any waste bins.

TEACHER: Mmm, they didn't have any waste bins.

DANIEL: They threw their rubbish into the gutter.

TEACHER: They threw their rubbish into the street, into an indentation just like a gutter. What else about the houses? Not only were they made of wood, they were—?

CLAIRE: Close together.

TEACHER: Yes, they were so close together, weren't they?

CLAIRE: You could—You could touch the other person's hand.

TEACHER: That's right, you could touch hands.

The teacher next signaled to the children that the text to be read was not in a story format, that it was a nonfiction book. That way, they were prepared for a reading that would not have the well-known structures of a story. (As indicated by the introduction, the children had heard other nonfiction works read by the teacher, and they were familiar with the term.)

TEACHER: Well, now I've found another book that's going to tell us about what happened a long time ago. And this is another nonfiction book about London, these are true stories about London. I'm going to read to you about what happened a long time ago. And it's [*reads*] "Fire! Fire!" And there's a picture of what we think it might have looked like when there was a big fire in London.

The teacher inserted the title into the comments that she was making about the book. She used changing intonation patterns to indicate when she was reading from the book and when she was making a comment.

CANDINA: It burnt a lot of the houses.

TEACHER: Yes, it burnt a lot of the houses, didn't it? Shall we find out? [*Reads*] "Fire was a frequent threat to the city of London." Why was it a threat?

CLAIRE: Because the fire could burn the people's houses down.

TEACHER: Why could it burn the houses down?

CANDINA: Because they were so close together.

TEACHER: So close together and they were made of—?

CHILDREN: Wood.

TEACHER: That's right. [*Continues reading*] "Since many London houses were wooden, fires could spread rapidly." They could spread quickly, couldn't they?

As the reading continued the number of comments made by the teacher suggested that, although the children had heard nonfiction read to them before, such readings had not been frequent. The teacher, therefore, made comments about the text and asked the children about the content probably as a means of ensuring that they were taking meaning from this more difficult expository genre. The teacher then continued by making a comment about the chronology of events, a concept the children might find difficult.

TEACHER: Then it tells us [*reads*] "In September 1666 . . ." What year are we now?

MICHAEL: Nineteen ninety-three.

TEACHER: Nineteen ninety-three. So this was over three hundred years ago, in 1666 [*resumes reading*] "the worst fire in London's history began in a baker's shop in Pudding Lane." And there's still a road in London called Pudding Lane. The baker's shop isn't there now, but the fire started in the baker's shop in Pudding Lane. [*Continues*] "Everything was dry after the long hot summer . . ." Everything was dry! " . . . and there was a strong wind"—I imagine a bit like today.

As with a story reading with young children the teacher took the opportunity of relating the text to the experiences of the children. The strong to gale-force winds that were buffeting London that day helped the teacher with the connection. Here, as elsewhere, in the information book reading, the teacher provided scaffolds to assist the children in their understanding of the ideas within the text and also, therefore, of the way in which the language was structured in order to present those ideas. But always the teacher was attempting to structure comments in order to lead back into the reading.

TEACHER: So if everything was all dry and there was a wind, what would happen to the fire?

KYLE: It would get bigger.

TEACHER: It would get bigger and bigger, yes. [*Reads*] ". . . so the flames leaped from house to house." Because of the wind it—

KYLE: —got bigger and bigger because it was dry.

TEACHER: Yes, it was all dry and the houses were made of—

CHILDREN: Wood.

TEACHER: And they were—

CHILDREN: Close together.

TEACHER: So the fire spread so quickly, but did they have big fire engines like we have today?

CHILDREN: No.

TEACHER: No. What would they have, do you think?

KYLE: Carts.

TEACHER: Carts.

MARTIN: Horses and water.

TEACHER: But what would the water be in?

KYLE: Pipes.

TEACHER: No, it wouldn't be in pipes like today.

LEE: In buckets.

TEACHER: In buckets, that's right. [*Continues*] "Chains of firefighters with buckets of water tried to stop the fire, but it was no use." You think what it would be like with buckets on a big house—not much use.

The teacher's reference to fire engines was another attempt to help the children bridge the three-hundred-year gap between the events being read about and the children's present context. Kyle's comment about moving the water through pipes demonstrated how difficult that task is with children of this age. Having reconfirmed the use of buckets, the teacher then continued with the reading.

TEACHER: "The fire raged for three days. On the fourth day the wind dropped. Dockworkers . . ." Who are dockworkers. Does anyone know?

SHAUN: They work near the sea on boats.

TEACHER: That's right, but where is London? Near the sea?

DANIEL: A river.

TEACHER: A river, that's right. Does anybody know the name?

ROBERT: The river Thames.

TEACHER: The river Thames, that's right. So the dockworkers who worked on the boats on the river Thames—do you know what they did to stop the fire? Well, this is what they did: they [*Reads*] "used gunpowder to blow up the streets of houses to make a big open space . . ." So if there's no houses . . .

SAMANTHA: And it couldn't go across the river.

TEACHER: And it couldn't go across the river. So that's how they stopped it. [*Reads*] "The city was saved."

GREG: What happened to all the people?

TEACHER: Well [*Continues*] "The homeless had to live in tents and huts in fields outside London until houses were built for them. Later that month King Charles"—that was the King who was on the throne in that time . . .

The teacher kept the reading going by using the comments from the children as a lead into the return to the text. Greg's question "What happened to all the people?" was especially helpful as it enabled the teacher to move straight into "The homeless. . . ." Subsequently, as it happened, an attempt to clarify the name of the current monarch was less successful than the teacher might have hoped. But that discussion was beneficial for the teacher because it gave further insights into the children's knowledge about the monarchy, and that information could be developed in another context with the children at a later date. That dialogue delayed, briefly, the completion of the reading.

TEACHER: Have we got a king at the moment?

CHILDREN: No.

TEACHER: Who have we got at the moment?

STACEY: Queen Victoria.

TEACHER: I don't think it's Queen Victoria. That's another queen a long time ago. What is our queen's name now?

RIKKY: Queen Elizabeth.

TEACHER: Queen Elizabeth. That's right. Well, Queen Elizabeth wasn't alive then, but King Charles was, and he [*Reads*] "made it law that houses were now to be built of brick or stone to help prevent fires." Why brick and stone?

LEE: Uh, in case there's another fire.

TEACHER: Right.

LEE: 'Cause it can't burn.

TEACHER: Because stone doesn't burn. But does wood?

CHILDREN: Yes.

The conclusion of the reading was designed to reassure the children about their own safety in their brick houses.

What is evident from this example is the similarity between that reading and storybook readings. The children were involved in the reading, they listened, they commented, and they responded. The teacher encouraged that involvement. The teacher also attempted to guide and facilitate the children's understanding of the text being read—perhaps a more difficult task with an expository text. But her reading of the book, her careful use of intonation and pauses, her acceptance of comments, and her own use of questions contributed to the children's understanding. And, as with story readings, it may be that later the children with more experience of such expository texts would be able to adopt more of a quiet listening role because they are able to reflect internally on the content.

However, although there were similarities between this nonfiction interaction and story reading interactions, there were differences in the text being read. The important question to be answered is "How might children be assisted in their understanding of expository books?" We assume that children benefit from hearing stories read aloud; it would seem reasonable to assume that that would also be the case for information books. Hearing a teacher read from information books enables children to detect differences in intontation patterns, vocabulary, sentences, meaning, and discourse patterns. Impersonal sentences such as "Fire was a frequent threat to the city of London" was best met first with support from a teacher. Such readings by the teacher give the children a model to work from when they meet such texts in the content areas.

Of course, information book readings are only a small part of the work in social studies or other content areas. Nevertheless, our example suggests that these readings support the children's learning to read from non-story books and ultimately, therefore, facilitates their reading to learn.

RUTH J. SÁEZ VEGA

"Los Niñitos Están Muy Preocupados por la Guerra": The Persian Gulf War in a Whole Language Kindergarten in Puerto Rico

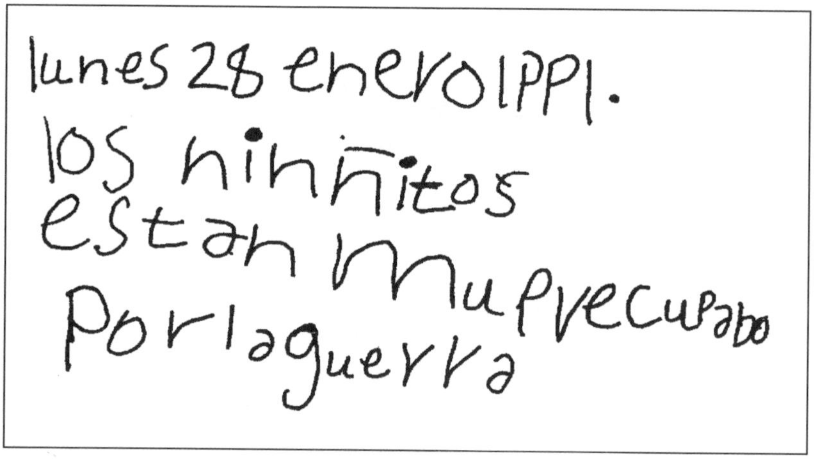

Figure 13–1

Los niñitos están muy preocupados por la guerra. The children are very concerned about the war.

IN AUGUST 1990 I WELCOMED A NEW GROUP OF KINDER-gartners to my classroom at the Escuela Elemental de la Universidad de Puerto Rico. This is a laboratory school that is part of the College of Education of the University of Puerto Rico. The children who come to my classroom are representative of a diversity of families and communities. They are selected from two groups: children whose parents are university employees, and children from the larger community.

As the children entered the classroom, their expressions demonstrated their enthusiasm. I was equally enthusiastic about working with them. As I do every year, I had spent much time planning and organizing my classroom. I wanted to make sure that all the children felt welcome. I wanted the classroom to be an inviting place, one the children felt a part of from the very first day. Pictures of the children had been placed at the door. As I greeted them, I asked them to pick out their picture and take it into the room with them. Each child was handed a clipboard with blank paper and a pencil. They were to sign in as they entered the room. Most of the children hugged and kissed their parents and said good-bye with excitement.

I strongly believe that the first week of class establishes the tone for the rest of the year. During that first week we spent time dialoguing in small groups. We were getting to know each other. We played many games, particularly games that dealt with building trust. We talked constantly.

The first part of each day throughout the year was spent in what I call "building community." It was a period of time in which we came together and sat in a circle on the floor. During this time we sang, talked, and informally greeted each other. I initiated dialogues by speaking about experiences I had on my way to school, news related to my family, news related to the children, current events, and the like. I wanted this to be a time for us to share, to get to know each other. I felt that as I spoke about myself and what was important to me, I demonstrated to the children that they could also share their experiences with the rest of us.

From the very first day the children knew they were able to express themselves freely. They began to share their personal lives and experiences, and we began to build a community. We talked about situations at school, at home, and in our country. We shared literature that had to do with such things as respect towards others, issues of diversity, conflict resolution, and expressions of feelings and emotions. We talked about solving conflicts peacefully. We dramatized conflicting situations and their possible solutions. We experienced and responded to literature in many ways. We read and discussed different versions of familiar stories. This allowed us to look at different perspectives to the same situation. We dramatized stories, painted murals, made masks, and wrote new scripts.

When a conflict arose in the room, children were helped to resolve it in peaceful ways. Occasionally, conflicts were dealt with by the class as a whole. At other times they were dealt with privately, among the people involved. I served as mediator. Children were encouraged to use words to express their ideas, feelings, and emotions. They were also encouraged to tell others what were the effects of their actions. Observing others and learning to read their facial expressions and other forms of nonverbal communication were highly encouraged.

As the year progressed children took upon themselves the role of mediators. In many circumstances no mediator was necessary, as the children themselves solved their own conflicts. Children were then encouraged to share with the group successful ways they had found of dealing with their conflicts. Of course, getting children to listen to each other and to be able to move from their points of view to those of others wasn't easy. However, with much dialogue and demonstration we were able to accomplish it.

Once I observed that Etienne and Armando had pulled two chairs to a private place in the classroom. I wasn't sure what was going on. From a distance it looked like a very serious meeting, and it was. As I walked towards them Armando looked at me and said, "Estamos hablando, estamos resolviendo un problema" (We're talking, we're solving a problem).

We had built a real classroom community, one in which people respected each other, one in which conflicts were dealt with in peaceful ways. The children had learned how to be empathetic to the feelings of others and how to listen to others with respect.

The War

In January 1991 the peaceful atmosphere in our classroom was threatened by a major event: the Persian Gulf War. Stress invaded the lives of many people, and my class was no exception. As the children came to school every day they talked constantly about the war. Some children had no notion of what the war meant, but many were worried and scared (and so was I). I wanted to help them deal with their fears as well as provide them with a variety of perspectives. As Jones and Berman (1991) have stated, "No matter how frightening some feelings are, it is far more frightening to think that no one is willing to talk about them" (p. 1). I felt I had a responsibility towards the children, to provide a forum for discussion.

> "La guerra me asusta" (The war frightens me).
>
> "Quiero que se acabe pronto" (I want it to end soon).
>
> "Anoche bombardearon a Israel" (Last night Israel was bombarded).
>
> "Murieron muchos niños" (Many children died).
>
> "No tienen comida" (They have no food).

These are only a few of the comments from my kindergarten students during the Persian Gulf War. The children in my classroom were not exempt from the feelings of fear and helplessness that the war brought about. Just as adults looked scared, worried, and stressed, so were the children. They demonstrated their feelings and emotions in a variety of ways.

As the coverage of the war continued, turmoil prevailed in our classroom. The children became hostile and aggressive towards others. The world was teaching the children that the use of violence is an acceptable way of dealing with problems. The children were solving their conflicts through the use of violence as well. Their behavior was far from what we had established at the beginning of the year. In fact, discipline became a major problem. We had to rethink possibilities for dealing with this as a group.

Besides their behavior becoming an issue, I knew that they had questions and misinformation about the war. I had many questions about the war myself. I believe in peace. I believe that as a world we need to look for more creative and peaceful solutions to our conflicts. I felt frustrated and helpless regarding the war. However, I hoped that in my classroom I could make a difference. I constantly asked myself: What has happened to the children's self-control? What should I do? How can I help them deal with this situation? How can I help them express their emotions regarding the war? How can I provide them with accurate information?

Searching for Answers

I got in touch with a few organizations for help. I engaged in extensive reading and dialogue with other educators. This had to be quick, for while I was searching for ways to help the children, the war continued. At first I looked for resources that dealt specifically with the issues of the Persian Gulf War. I wanted to be able to engage in a natural dialogue with the children, but at the same time I wanted to avoid being led exclusively by my emotions and beliefs regarding the war.

With the advances of modern technology we were able to watch the war in the comfort of our own homes. The media had portrayed this event with a total lack of humanity. Our children saw this televised "show." In many ways it was no different from the movies and cartoons they regularly watch on TV— except that this time it was real! I needed to help clarify some of the children's fantasies regarding the war. It was not a video game, although it may have seemed like it on television.

Some children had seen relatives leave to take part in the war. Other children knew about other Puerto Rican men and women leaving, from what they had seen on TV. They listened and observed. They talked about the war constantly. It was evident that they were not only ready, they needed to talk about it.

We spent much time in large and small groups. A mixture of emotions was evident—fear, anxiety, confusion—yet everyone knew the war was taking place. Everyone talked about it. I had to help them explore their feelings. My main role was that of a listener and a watcher. I saw this as a further opportunity to help the children learn how to listen and respond to others in caring ways. During our daily morning discussions I was attentive to nonverbal signs. Young children are not always able to express their feelings with words, but their facial expressions, posture, and gestures make clear their feelings.

The media's portrayal of the war made it important for me to help the children distinguish reality from fantasy. In providing accurate information to counter their misconceptions I was guided by the recommendations given by Educators for Social Responsibility (Jones and Berman 1991). I responded to the obvious terms of the misinformation, answered questions in simple and straightforward terms, and kept my responses brief and simple. I provided factual answers based on each child's understanding and made sure that I didn't give them more information than necessary. I tried to respond to the children in ways that were supportive of them.

One day as we were talking about the conflict, Jorge initiated a major discussion when he commented: "Yo no entiendo porqué Hussein y Bush tienen que pelear. ¿Es que ellos no saben hablar como nosotros? ¿Es que no saben que los problemas se resuelven hablando, y no con la violencia?" (I don't understand why Hussein and Bush have to fight. Is it that they don't know how to talk, like we do? Don't they know that problems are solved through talking, not through violence?) Other children responded immediately to Jorge's genuine concern. They shared their opinions on this matter. Some like Jorge expressed their inability to understand the nature of the war. Others offered possible alternatives to an armed conflict. Among their solutions were to engage in dialogue, to have mediators, and to throw away all war "toys."

Making it Real

Our discussions on the war brought about an interest in the news from a different perspective. The newspaper became a major focus of our literacy and play. We used it every day in our classroom. Reading the paper for the news on the war grew to reading other news, as well as articles, advertisements, and so forth.

We visited a major newspaper publishing company, where we followed the process of publishing a newspaper. After that our dramatic play area became a newspaper office. We had telephones, newspapers, pictures, and of course lots of plain newsprint paper (donated by the local newspaper). We decided to make a mural newspaper, *El Periódico del Kinder*, which would consist of news about our classroom. Our newspaper reflected the variety of news published in any newspaper. There were different sections and types of news: announcements, warnings, socials, reports on current events, and the like. Many children wrote (or dictated) their pieces in the third person, even when they themselves were involved in the event. They were aware that a newspaper is not a collection of stories, it is a different genre.

A news broadcast was also set up in our classroom. A group of older children made a television out of a large cardboard box. The kindergartners set up a broadcast and reported on the daily news. Their broadcast included local news, sports, cultural events, weather, and of course news on the war and the war zone. Much writing took place as the reporters wrote their news before they went on the air. Figure 13-2 presents examples of news reports written by the children.

The children decided they wanted to visit a television studio and watch a news broadcast. They chose a particular channel because it was the only channel in which there was an interpreter for the deaf, who presented the news in sign language. In our classroom we learned, used, and valued sign language, as it helped us communicate with a group of hard of hearing children who frequently visited us.

While at the television station the children were invited to participate in the filming of "peace news," a simulated news broadcast. As I observed the children I noticed that their "news reporting" focused on one viewpoint of the war. They mentioned

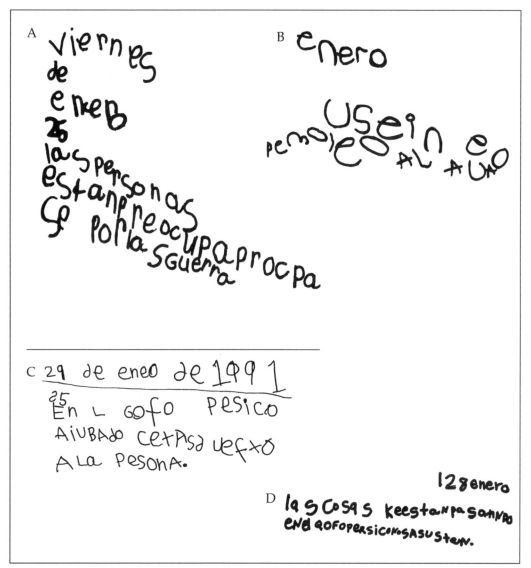

Figure 13–2

News Reports Written by the Children. A: "Las personas están preocupándose por la guerra" (People are getting worried about the war). B: "Hussein echó petróleo al agua" (Hussein threw oil into the water). C: "En el Golfo Pérsico hay un bombardeo que está afectando a las personas" (There is a bombing at the Persian Gulf that is affecting the people). D: "Las cosas que están pasando en el Golfo Pérsico nos asustan" (The things that are happening at the Persian Gulf scare us).

how the people in Puerto Rico felt happy because the war was over and talked about the involvement of Puerto Rican relatives in the war. They neglected anything that had to do with the people in the area of the conflict.

"What have I done?" I thought. The children were able to understand that the war was not a game. They knew that it was real and that people suffered and died. However, we needed to move a step further. In being so concerned with supporting the children through the war, I had missed an essential aspect of peace education. I wanted my children to understand, to the extent that it is possible when you are five or six years old, the consequences of the war on the people and the environment at the war zone.

One Step Further

That evening I read, and I spoke to a colleague, Anaida Pascual Morán. Anaida is a peace educator. She and I were members of a study group on peace education. Wichert (1989) has addressed the importance of dialogue in peace education, indicating that reflection is not enough, that we need to dialogue with others on these issues. Dialoguing helps us clarify our thoughts. Anaida helped me think through the process. Together we analyzed what was happening in my classroom and explored ways to proceed.

Back in the classroom I initiated an honest dialogue with the children. We talked about their news broadcast and analyzed it. According to Jones and Berman (1991), "in age-appropriate ways" we can help children see "the human and environmental consequences for all sides" (p. 3). Together we began to explore possibilities for learning about the people of the Middle East as well as the effects of the war on the people and the environment.

The children had many questions about the life in the Middle East. Their questions guided our inquiry. We gathered resources: books, journals, newspapers, pictures, videos, and so on. As we looked at their contents, we soon discovered that most of our resources perpetuated stereotypes instead of providing a realistic, human point of view. Rather than discard these resources, we used them as the basis for discussions that allowed the children to become aware of prejudice and stereotypes. For example, by that time the news broadcasts were airing reports on life in the Middle East. In our classroom we compared and contrasted the contents of these reports with information from other sources.

Some children were interested in looking at the differences and similarities between the people of the Middle East and ourselves. Others were interested in the desert and the animals of the desert. We studied similarities and differences with our own environment. Some children wanted to study the environmental consequences of the war. This topic led us to discuss other ways in which humans have threatened the environment, particularly those that affect Puerto Rico. The children and I learned about how we are polluting our environment by tearing down our forests and by contaminating the bodies of water within and surrounding our island.

When the war came to an end, the children were relieved to know that it was over. However, their interest in studying the environment and its protection that had evolved from the study of the war continued as a major focus of the class throughout the rest of the semester. Our year culminated with an in-depth study on the protection of the environment. At the end of the year, as was the tradition in my classroom, the children and I planned a celebration of our shared experiences in kindergarten. Stories, poems, and songs were joined together by a script created in collaboration between the children and myself. Every child participated. Parents and friends joined us in what became a tribute to the environment and a call for its protection.

Looking Back

As teachers, no matter how much we prepare for a school year, we cannot foresee catastrophes, such as war. I wasn't ready to deal within my kindergarten classroom with the issue of the war. However, as terrible as it was, it was part of what our world was going through. As a teacher I could not ignore it, and I certainly could not teach ignoring the world. I believe that if I truly want my students to live in a more just and peaceful society, I have the responsibility to give them the tools to build such a world. I have the responsibility to educate them for peace. As Pascual Morán (1989) notes, we should take current world conflicts as basic references for peace education.

I am not sure, and I guess I never will be, exactly what my students took from this experience. However, if, by doing what we did, there will be more people who believe in searching for peaceful and creative alternatives to solving conflicts and protecting our environment, then the goal was accomplished.

De la misma forma que la guerra empieza en la mente del hombre, la paz comienza en nuestras mentes. El mismo ser que inventó la guerra puede inventar la paz. La responsabilidad radica en cada uno de nosotros.

Declaración sobre la Violencia
Sevilla, 16 de mayo de 1986

Just as war starts in the minds of men, peace also starts in our minds. The same being that invented war can invent peace. The responsibility is within each and every one of us.

Declaration on Violence,
Seville, May 16, 1986

14

KATHLEEN CRAWFORD   MARGARET FERGUSON
GLORIA KAUFFMAN   JULIE LAIRD
JEAN SCHROEDER   KATHY G. SHORT

Exploring Historical and Multicultural Perspectives Through Inquiry

WHEN WE WERE STUDENTS, SOCIAL STUDIES CLASS MEANT reading textbooks, filling out worksheets, coming up with "right" answers in class discussions, and taking tests about dates and events that we forgot as soon as the test was over. Research consisted of copying information on assigned topics from the encyclopedia into a nice booklet to hand in to the teacher. We spent a lot of time "covering" many topics and facts and ended up with only superficial knowledge about, or interest in, those topics.

In recent years, along with many other teachers, we moved from textbook-dominated approaches to theme units. Instead of textbooks, our students read fiction and nonfiction and engaged in a wide range of activities related to those books and the social studies themes we were studying. Students were encouraged to share what they knew on a particular topic and what they wanted to know. They were involved in problem solving as they researched topics related to the theme and prepared projects to share with classmates (Short and Armstrong 1993).

While we found theme units to be interesting and motivating for students, we wanted to create even more powerful connections and so began to explore inquiry. We wanted to *integrate* curriculum around concepts and issues, rather than *correlate* different subject areas to a particular topic. Instead of creating activities from books, we wanted to put our focus on inquiry and use literature to support that inquiry. Most important, we wanted our students not only to be problem-solvers, but to become problem-posers, able to pose and explore their own questions (Freire 1985). We realized that our students needed more time to find questions of significance to them. They needed longer to "wander and wonder" (Short 1993) within a particular topic before moving on to research. Because our focus had been on problem-solving, students either researched their own factual questions, which often lacked depth, or they accepted teacher topics and questions. We knew that for inquiry to become a powerful part of the classroom, we needed to find ways to support students in finding and exploring questions that mattered in their lives and worlds.

The move from thematic to inquiry approaches in social studies has not been an easy change for us. In this chapter, we want to share our journey in a one-year teacher research project. We will begin with a description of why we came together as a group and an overview of what happened in each classroom. We will then discuss three major issues that ran through our different experiences and provide classroom examples of these issues. Examples will come from Julie's kindergarten, Margaret's first grade, Jean's primary multi-age, Kathleen's fourth grade, Gloria's fifth grade, and Kathy's graduate course.

Building a Teacher Research Community

Our initial questions as teachers about inquiry and children grew out of a university course in which we discussed issues related to the Columbus Quincentenary, specifically how to provide multiple historical perspectives and whether to present harsh historical events to young children. Later, in a seminar on research in children's literature, we read studies that indicated that young children have difficulty understanding history (Levstik and Pappas 1987) and that they are egocentric and unable to consider perspectives other than their own (Piaget 1977). We believed that these studies examined young children's understandings in settings that did not support them in developing a sense of history or in considering the perspectives of others around them. We wanted to challenge this notion by building powerful classroom contexts for inquiry. We formed a teacher research group to examine our questions about children's multicultural and historical understandings.

Because of our questions and the Columbus Quincentenary, we decided to weave our broad concept of discovery across each of our classrooms. Our research group met to begin "planning to plan" (Watson, Burke, and Harste 1989) over the spring and summer. We webbed possible inquiries that might develop from discovery and put together text sets of five to ten conceptually related books (see Figure 14–1) around such topics as living in harmony with nature, navigation and mapmaking, ownership, perspectives on the Columbus voyages, greed, and cultural encounters (Short et al. 1992). We continued meeting every other week during the year to discuss how we were working through this broad concept and supporting inquiry in each of our classrooms.

We all began the year with the same broad focus on discovery and an exploration of personal and family histories, but

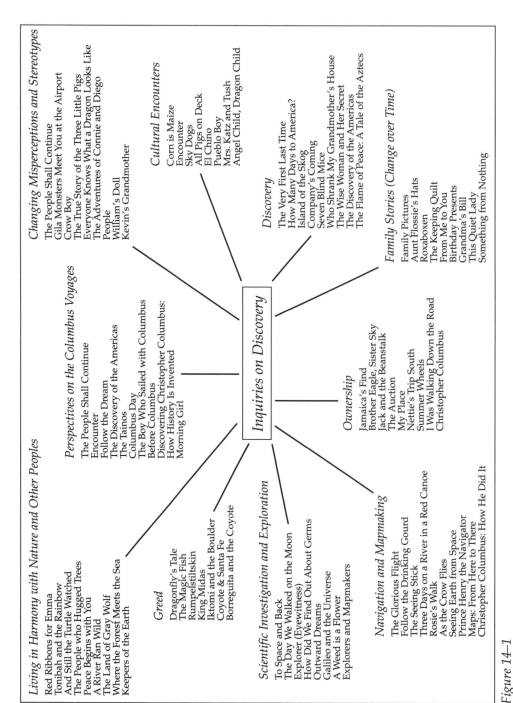

Figure 14–1
Web of Possibilities for Discovery Text Sets

each classroom took on different inquiries based on student and teacher interests. Julie's kindergarten class moved from discovery and family stories into an exploration of change over time. The students were intrigued with the many family stories that depicted characters growing from babies to children to adults with their own babies, thus starting the cycle over again. They made continuous use of time lines to develop a sense of history and as one way of ordering events in time. Margaret's first-grade students also focused on discovering how things change over time. They were interested in changes in families and places, especially the change that occurs when another group "discovers" a particular place. The students moved from families to studies of different biomes around the world and then back to individual family histories.

In Jean's multi-age classroom of first, second, and third graders, the first half of the year was spent developing concepts of history and time lines and exploring the discovery text sets as part of wandering and wondering. During the spring, they formed inquiry groups to pursue focused questions on a wide range of social and scientific issues, such as the history of bugs, Jean's childhood, and boat building. Kathleen's fourth-grade students focused their explorations of discovery around understanding and learning how to accept each other and their various cultures. They became aware of the treatment of American Indians in Arizona and connected that learning to accepting peoples from other cultures, especially those represented by the children in the classroom.

In fifth grade, Gloria's students began with a focus on building community that led to explorations of text sets related to time, perspective, and change. Their discussions of books on Columbus and the discovery text sets brought up issues of culture, religion, and human rights. They were particularly interested in using multiple perspectives to understand the rights of animals, various ethnic groups, and children. The graduate students in Kathy's class, most of whom were teachers, also talked about the rights of children, but their concern was providing children with multiple perspectives from which to understand history instead of protecting children from harsh events. Inaccurate and one-sided accounts of the Columbus events led them to question much of what they had learned as students and taught as teachers about American history. They began to search for books that reflected multiple perspectives on that history.

As we shared and compared what was happening in our classrooms, several major issues came up frequently. These three issues will provide the framework for the rest of this chapter: weaving broad concepts throughout the year to support continuous inquiry; exploring ways to engage students in "wandering and wondering" as a way of focusing inquiry questions; and finding ways to support focused inquiry.

Weaving Broad Concepts Through Our Inquiries

Two broad frameworks wove across each of our classrooms. For all of us, the inquiry cycle (Short 1993) provided a powerful curriculum framework that we could use in planning curriculum with our students (see Figure 14–2).

The second framework was provided by the use of the broad concept of discovery to connect and integrate our experiences throughout the year. For us, a broad concept is one students can use to connect a wide range of topics and ideas. It does not limit the focus of class and student inquiry, but simply provides a sense of connection. When we used themes such as community helpers or the Civil War across the entire day, the connections often seemed trite and forced. In contrast, broad concepts, such as cycles, change, and discovery, provide many possible points of connection that naturally weave across the day and year and do not limit the topics and questions students can pursue. We each began the year by exploring discovery, encouraging students to discover new things about their rooms, schools, selves, classmates, and families. We then used these experiences to reflect on the concept of discovery.

Developing Concepts About Discovery

In all of the classrooms, we began the fall with engagements in which students discovered new things about each other. Several classrooms used the strategy "Getting to Know You" (Harste, Short, and Burke 1988), where students interviewed each other and wrote articles for a class newspaper from these interviews. Kindergarten students found out about each other through

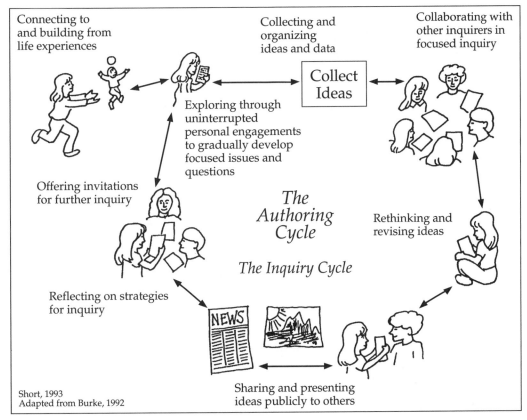

Connecting to and building from life experiences

Collecting and organizing ideas and data

Collaborating with other inquirers in focused inquiry

Collect Ideas

Exploring through uninterrupted personal engagements to gradually develop focused issues and questions

Offering invitations for further inquiry

The Authoring Cycle

Rethinking and revising ideas

The Inquiry Cycle

Reflecting on strategies for inquiry

NEWS

Sharing and presenting ideas publicly to others

Short, 1993
Adapted from Burke, 1992

Figure 14–2
The Inquiry Cycle

surveys on each other's favorite foods, colors, and so forth. At the university, students participated in a Literacy Dig (Taylor 1990): they went through their wallets or purses to find evidence of the ways in which they use reading and writing. They shared these digs with each other in small groups as a way to learn something new about others.

Students also explored their environment. On Registration Day, Margaret invited students and parents to discover the classroom by choosing a place to sit and participating in several discovery centers to encourage them to feel ownership of the room. In several classrooms, students wandered around the school or the classroom and then came together to web what they had discovered. Another way in which discovery was highlighted was through exploring science as an inquiry process. After reading *Mr. Archimedes' Bath* (Allen 1980), multi-age students participated in a water displacement experiment, recorded the results, explored other accounts of this concept, and talked about the broader methods of scientific inquiry. Fourth graders' observations of the reaction between watercolor and rubbing alcohol or salt also led to a discussion of the processes of scientific inquiry. Fifth graders participated in field events, recording data, creating graphs, and sharing discoveries of their athletic abilities.

The concept of discovery was then woven through the different topics that whole groups, small groups, and individuals explored, not through direct lessons, but through conversations and occasional connections. Each classroom developed different understandings about discovery because of differences in student interests and questions. Both kindergarten and first-grade students focused on discovery as change over time, while multi-age students were more interested in history and exploration. Fourth graders, fifth graders, and university students were interested in discovery as understanding multiple perspectives.

Each classroom developed a web or chart in which children brainstormed their understandings about discovery (see Figure 14–3). Stephanie, a first grader, stated, "Discover means a lot to me. Discovery means I found something out that I never knew." Jake added, "Discovery is power." The multi-age students distinguished between three kinds of discovery on their webs: finding something that nobody knows about, finding something that others know about but you have not found before, and going back to something and finding something you didn't see the first time. Fifth graders talked about discovery as a process of deciding on "something you want to find out about and then doing research." Elan, a kindergarten child, added a note of caution: "You have to be quiet when you discover something so you don't scare it away."

FLOWING FROM ONE INQUIRY TO ANOTHER

The concept of discovery became a thread that allowed one inquiry to flow into the next. We had expected to finish our focus on discovery by December, but found that it actually ended only because the last day of school arrived. The topics pursued in the

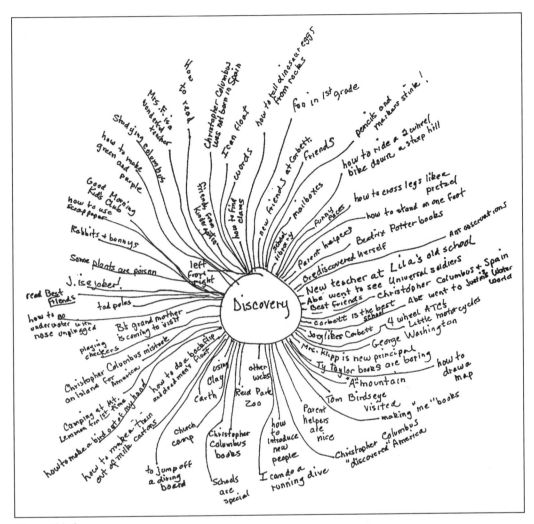

Figure 14–3
First-Grade Web of Concept of Discovery

classrooms came from a variety of sources including the children, teachers, and the school curriculum. No matter where the
topic originated, however, we were concerned that the questions
explored within these topics come from the children.

In some cases, the broad class focus was initiated by the students, not the teacher. From the first week of school, the multi-age

students wanted to know which seas were the "seven seas." Although Jean showed no interest in this question, the children pursued it and eventually an inquiry group formed to figure out what really were the seven seas and whether Columbus had actually sailed them.

In other cases, the broad focus was initiated by the teacher. While Kathy introduced the topic of Columbus into her course and provided engagements to support exploration of this topic, she did not impose her questions onto the group. The discussions and engagements invited open-ended responses, out of which major questions developed about protection versus perspective.

Even though we teachers sometimes initiated the broad focus, we listened carefully to student interests and questions and used them to plan engagements that would allow students to explore these in greater depth. During a discussion of Columbus, Gloria read aloud *Encounter* (Yolen 1992). Instead of focusing on the Columbus event, the fifth graders were interested in understanding culture and whether someone can take your culture away from you. Their questions led Gloria to choose *The Devil's Arithmetic* (Yolen 1988) as the next read-aloud. During class discussions of this book, the issues of rights and cultures were raised over and over, so Gloria put together shared book sets (multiple copies of the same title) to support small-group discussions of these issues.

In still other cases, the broad focus or topic was mandated by the school curriculum. Kathleen found a way to support both the students' questions and the state-mandated curriculum on Arizona history, geography, and culture. She decided to bring in shared book sets on issues related to American Indians in Arizona, because students had raised these issues as they explored the discovery text sets.

Engaging in Wandering and Wondering

Previously, most of us had asked students what they knew and wanted to know at the beginning of a unit. Because the questions students were able to ask at this point were often factually based, they did not provide a powerful context for inquiry. As we examined our own inquiry processes, we realized that often we spend as much time trying to find our questions as we do actually researching those questions. We began to think about how we might better support our students in wandering and wondering as they explored different perspectives and information on a topic and gradually posed significant questions that connected to their own lives and world.

Supporting Wandering and Wondering

Wandering and wondering provides many experiences with "doing" as students read, write, talk, observe, interview, and explore a topic broadly. The goal is to allow them to answer their initial factual questions, build greater understanding of the topic from a broader range of perspectives, and gradually move to problem posing and focused inquiry. Even though it was not our initial plan, the discovery text sets became an important part of wandering and wondering. We had put the discovery text sets together to support focused inquiry, but we made the mistake of having students form groups to discuss these sets without giving them time to pose their own questions and issues. Because students did not have questions that led them to need these sets to support their inquiry, the sets became part of their wandering and wondering and they used them for browsing and sharing rather than dialogue and inquiry.

The wandering and wondering process sometimes lasted only a day or two and other times lasted several months. Sometimes literature played a key role in this process; at other times, hands-on experiences were more crucial. For several days, kindergartners observed crickets in a dry aquarium and then put them in small jars for a closer look. These observations were shared in class discussions and led to questions about insect body parts, which then became a class focus for inquiry. As part of a rain forest study, first graders spent two weeks in the library gathering books, maps, charts, and artifacts that they used to form their own text sets. As they browsed and discussed these text sets, they began to develop their own questions for inquiry. In fifth grade, the experiences of the entire first semester with read-alouds and literature circles on discovery, conflict, change over time, family, and Columbus led to questions and in-depth inquiry about cultures, rights, and beliefs during the second semester.

FINDING A SIGNIFICANT QUESTION

While the wandering and wondering encouraged students to think more broadly about a topic, we were also concerned that they gradually find an issue or question that would take them into more focused inquiry. We found that these questions emerged from a variety of sources and were supported in different ways within the classroom. Kathy supported graduate students in finding questions by having them record their questions, issues, and interests on brainstorming charts and webs as they wandered and wondered. When fourth graders encountered difficulty exploring their questions, Kathleen adapted Carolyn Burke's focused study approach (1992) and presented it by having the class engage in a mini-inquiry using a whole-class text set on change over cultures, which they used to guide their own small-group inquiries.

Often students' questions changed as they explored their initial interests and gained more experience. In the multi-age classroom, an inquiry group on the history of bugs had difficulty finding information to answer their question of "Who was the first person to ever find the first bug that ever existed?" Their inquiry took a different direction as they became interested in information about specific bugs and the ways farmers control infestation. When Julie first read aloud several family stories on change over time such as *Window* (Baker 1991) and *This Quiet Lady* (Zolotow 1992), the kindergarten students did not understand some of these books. However, when she reread them later in the year after they'd learned more about change over time in families, they asked many questions about age and cycles of life within families. Their questions changed because they brought more experiences and understandings to the books.

Sometimes questions changed because of particular engagements. As a small group of fifth graders discussed *Mississippi Bridge* (Taylor 1990) in a literature circle, they wondered whether blacks and whites could respect each other. Their literature discussion led them into a focused inquiry on civil rights, which involved library research and an interview with an African American teacher in the building. Early in the year, first-grade students played a get-acquainted game that involved finding someone who spoke another language. This game led to questions about different languages and an interest in language diversity that continued throughout the school year.

While we supported students in examining their own questions, we also pushed them to consider other questions and to think in critical ways. A group in the multi-age classroom wanted to know what Jean was like when she was little. She encouraged them to expand their questions to also consider what the world was like at that time. She did not reject their question, but pushed them to broaden it to include other societal issues. After reading about Columbus and the attempted enslavement of American Indians, fifth graders engaged in an in-depth inquiry on African Americans and slavery. When Gloria brought in a newspaper article about slavery in the world today, students could no longer consider slavery as something from the past, and they began to look at their own social responsibilities.

Engaging in Focused Inquiry

As students moved into focused inquiry, they needed collaborative experiences with other inquirers where they could think together about their issues and questions. Often these experiences involved the use of literature as well as other primary sources. Students also needed to use various tools, such as time lines and webs, to help them collect and organize their information and ideas so they did not become overwhelmed and could see patterns in what they were finding.

USING LITERATURE TO SUPPORT INQUIRY

In their collaborative groups, we found that literature played very different roles in students' inquiries. They used literature as the central focus of their inquiry, as another reference source, or as part of a related study. When literature was central to the inquiry, it became the major focus for allowing students to think through their questions and issues. They met to discuss and explore this literature in depth through either whole-class discussions or small-group literature circles on text sets and shared book sets (Short and Klassen 1993). These literature circles were the heart of their inquiry and went from conversations to dialogue on issues of great importance to them.

The kindergarten whole-class literature discussions on shared books about change over time often provided students with an opportunity to delve into concepts such as old age and to sort out their understanding of time in their own lives. Kathleen read aloud from a text set on cultural encounters and exchanges in such books as *Encounter* (Yolen 1992) and *How My Parents Learned to Eat* (Friedman 1984) to fourth graders over several weeks. The students made a list of issues that most concerned them (see Figure 14–4), and Kathleen put together text sets from these issues that students used for small-group literature circles and further inquiry.

When fifth graders began asking questions about rights, Gloria supported their inquiries by providing each group with a shared book on the rights of a particular group. For example, the inquiry group focusing on animal rights and abuse read *Shiloh* (Naylor 1991) and the group focusing on slavery read *From Slave to Abolitionist* (Warner 1993). In Kathy's graduate course, students read and discussed two books about Columbus

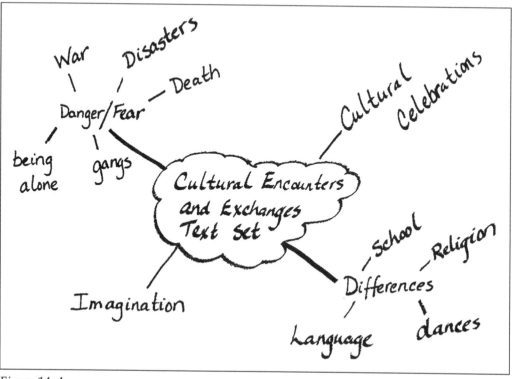

Figure 14–4
Fourth-Grade Web of Issues Related to Cultural Encounters and Exchanges

in whole- and small-group discussions. These books formed an important context from which students then developed small-group and individual inquiries on a wide range of issues.

The nature of students' questions and inquiries determined the kinds of resources they needed for doing research and for reaching new understandings and questions. Sometimes literature was not central to their inquiry, but became part of a larger set of resources they explored. In this case, students used books as references to find specific pieces of information or establish a background context but did not engage in intensive discussion of the issues they contained.

Most of the small groups in the multi-age class used literature as a reference because their topics did not lend themselves to literature discussion. The group interested in boat building began their inquiry with a shared book set of *How a House Is Built* (Gibbons 1990) because Jean could find so few books on boat building and wanted to connect their inquiry to more familiar processes. The group added many books on boats to create a reference set for their inquiry. The group studying Jean as a little girl primarily used interviews and childhood artifacts, but they also read some of Jean's favorite childhood stories and a book about the polio epidemic in her hometown.

During a temperate forest biome study, first graders studied New Zealand. They became interested in the Maoris, especially how they were treated by the Europeans who came to that country. They compared this to the treatment of American Indians, leading them to develop a reference text set on American Indians. In the university course, the many questions about Columbus led to a constantly expanding text set of books, articles, editorials, and maps about the Columbus event from a variety of perspectives. This set was kept at the back of the room and used as a reference set throughout a wide range of inquiries. When students broke into groups to explore related topics such as Native American perspectives on life, the Renaissance, mapmaking, navigation, and picture books on Columbus, they put together text sets to serve as references for their brainstorming of possible topics and classroom engagements.

Sometimes literature was used as part of students' inquiries. These books had an influence on the students' inquiries, but were not central to them and were often used by different groups of students. As fourth graders engaged in small-group literature circles on chapter books about Arizona, Kathleen read aloud Byrd Baylor's books for a whole-class author study. Jean often put related books at the listening center, such as *The Ugly Duckling* (Moore 1987) when students were considering change over time. While her students continued to work in their inquiry groups, Jean also created shared book sets of historical fiction and biographies. Children selected a book they wanted to read and discuss and met in new literature groups that involved different students than their inquiry groups.

SEARCHING FOR PRIMARY SOURCES

Literature was one source for students' inquiries, but there were many other sources of information that students used to support their inquiries. Initially we had focused on history as the story of famous people and events, but gradually we came to realize that history involves a process of research and the use of particular tools and resources, and that this process is much more important to children's understanding of history than a list of facts about events and people. In particular, we were concerned that students have access to primary sources and have the chance to interpret history from those sources. These primary sources became important as children realized that the history they were reading was based on someone's perspective. Unless they knew something about the primary sources used by that author, they could not be sure of the accuracy or perspective of that book.

People served as one valuable primary source. Children interviewed class members, their teachers, other teachers in the building, families, and guest speakers. Multi-age students interviewed Jean as part of their inquiry about her childhood. Fourth graders talked with foster children from their classroom as part of their discussion of *The Pinballs* (Byars 1977). In all of the classrooms, children interviewed family members as sources for personal time lines and family stories. Fifth graders developed questions and tape-recorded an interview with an African American teacher. Kindergartners asked a guest speaker from the zoo questions about how to solve problems they were having with birds eating the plants from their garden. First graders were interested in how to write for publication and so invited a newspaper reporter to speak to them.

When children could not interview people directly, they wrote letters. In the multi-age classroom, the history of space group wrote to the National Air and Space Museum, the boat group wrote to a boat building company, the group focusing on Jean wrote to her family, the bug group wrote to a parent studying agriculture and to the university's entomology department, and the seven seas group wrote to the Smithsonian.

Another primary source was actual observation. Margaret took her students to the Tucson Botanical Gardens to research their questions about layers of foliage and aerial roots in rain forests. Gloria and her fifth graders visited Hohokam ruins so they could research their questions about ancient peoples.

Artifacts from particular time periods and cultures served as an additional primary source for historical research. The boat group built a model of a dinghy so they could understand the boat building process. In the university course, students examined the journals of Columbus as a primary document, but found through further research that the original journals were lost and only adaptations were available.

USING A BROAD RANGE OF TOOLS

Because of our new awareness of the historical research process, we encouraged students to use a much broader range of tools and procedures than had been present in our classrooms previously. Literature and learning logs had always been our major resources, but with the changing focus of the students' questions, we found it necessary to look at historians and learn from their processes and tools for inquiry. As students explored primary sources and literature, they needed tools that would allow them to collect and organize information and ideas and share these ideas with others.

One of the major tools explored by our students was the time lines. In all of the classrooms, students constructed personal and family time lines (see Figure 14–5). To create a physical sense of a five-hundred-year span of time, multi-age students hung a two-hundred-fifty-foot rope from the hallway ceilings and first graders used five hundred one-inch wooden beads. Significant dates and events were added to these time lines throughout the year. The kindergarten students made time lines from read-aloud books on how families change over time. At the end of the year, they constructed a time line history of the year from their daily class journal.

Graphs were another important tool for collecting information. Kindergarten and first-grade students used graphs to

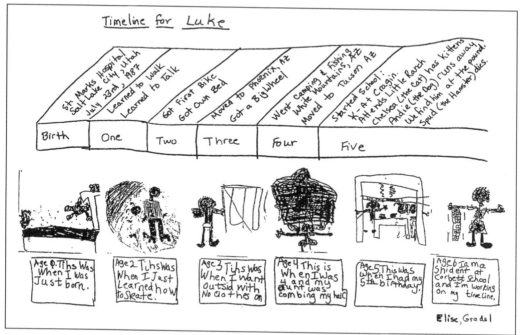

Figure 14–5
Kindergarten and First-Grade Personal Timelines

record their surveys on personal likes and dislikes such as favorite foods, colors, TV shows, and clothing. The seven seas group in the multi-age classroom developed a survey on the different meanings of the phrase "sailing the seven seas" and graphed the results. Maps were a valuable source of information for the university students who were exploring oceans, navigation, and mapmaking in their small-group inquiries.

Webs were another organizational tool that cut across all of our classrooms because they provided a visual way to capture and organize brainstorming about our learning, connections, and questions. In the university course, students used webs to brainstorm connections and issues related to discovery. They also created "webs of possibilities" as they worked on their small-group themes. They used these webs to brainstorm possible topics related to their theme and to list related books and classroom activities. Sometimes students began with graffiti boards—chart paper where they wrote and sketched ideas and connections. These were later organized into a web within their small groups. Fifth graders made extensive use of webs to brainstorm and record significant issues and connections in their literature circles.

Webs and lists were also used as ways to help students keep track of their questions. Kathleen and Gloria had their students record their questions in their literature logs. Margaret and Jean created class and individual lists of questions that carried across the year (see Figure 14–6). As new questions arose, they were added to the list. At various times, students used these lists to create inquiry groups, where they would pursue some of these questions in more depth. Many questions were lost until we came up with ways of capturing them as they arose in discussions and explorations.

Note taking was an important tool that students needed to use during their inquiries. As they interviewed family members, they took notes, which they later shared orally in the class and then used in writing stories and constructing time lines. They also used notes for the "Getting to Know You" activity and interviewing guests.

Logs were another type of written record kept by students. Julie, Margaret, and Jean all kept some type of daily class log in their rooms to record the history of their year. First-grade students found Columbus's use of a public and personal journal fascinating and began keeping a public class journal as well as personal journals. Many of us used learning logs or literature logs, in which students reflected daily on their learning and reading, as well as portfolios, where students reflexively examined what and how they were learning several times a year.

As students shared their research with others, they explored many ways to present their thinking to others. Sometimes they shared informally by telling about their research and what they had learned using webs and other artifacts they had created in the process. Other groups spent time putting together more formal presentations that they shared with classmates, other classrooms, and/or parents. Their presentations included class books and individual books, mime, plays, original opera, choral reading, murals, songs with signing, music, graphics on overheads, costumes, masks, square dancing, displays, oral presentations, quilts, even bird feeders. In their presentations, they found creative ways to share what they had learned as well as the processes they had used to explore their questions.

Conclusion

At the end of the year, each of us reflected with our students and with each other on what had been most significant about our study of discovery and inquiry. Julie's kindergarten students showed tremendous growth in gaining a sense of time and in their understanding of the cyclical quality of life. They also had learned how to go about researching their questions. Margaret's

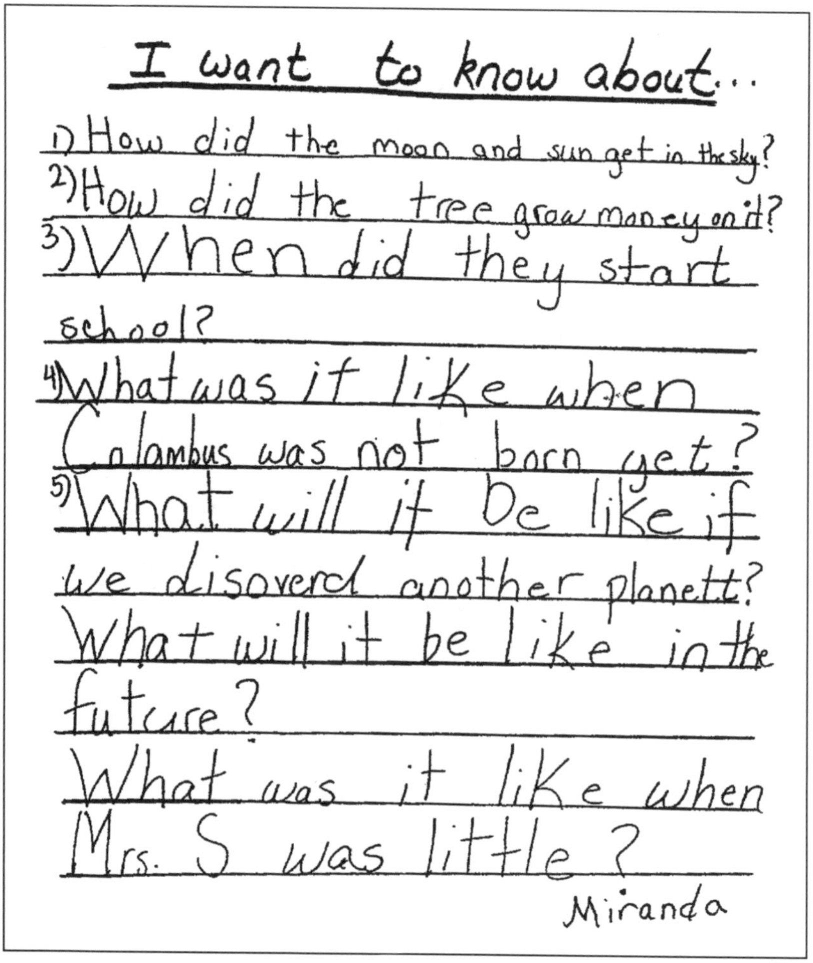

Figure 14–6
Individual Lists of
Questions from
Multi-Age Class

I want to know about...

1) How did the moon and sun get in the sky?
2) How did the tree grow money on it?
3) When did they start school?
4) What was it like when Colambus was not born yet?
5) What will it be like if we disoverd another planett?
What will it be like in the future?
What was it like when Mrs. S was little?

Miranda

first-grade students saw inquiry as giving them permission to be in charge of their own learning. As they reflected on their learning in their portfolios, they saw how they had changed over time and were able to evaluate their own learning instead of being dependent on the teacher's judgments. Gaining a sense of independence was also important in Jean's multi-age classroom. Students realized that they knew how to conduct their own research through interviewing on the telephone, setting up their own visitors for the classroom, finding resources in the library, and writing letters. Students had gained a strong understanding of historical research through their use of primary sources and time lines.

Kathleen's fourth-grade students learned how to respect each other and accept one another for who they were. When Gerald was able to share his expertise about Malcolm X and Martin Luther King, Jr., in his literature circle, he gained the respect of the group members in ways that carried beyond the group. Gloria's fifth-grade students came to appreciate and value both the universal qualities shared by all peoples and the differences that make each group and person distinct. They developed a critical viewpoint on their reading and interactions with outside experts. They realized that books and people have a particular perspective and tell only one part of any story. This critical viewpoint was also important in Kathy's graduate course as many teachers realized that history was not just a set of facts, but a particular perspective that needed to be balanced with other ways of seeing the world. They ended the course with many questions about inquiry and how to support their students in finding and exploring their own questions.

As we reflected together, we realized that all of our students gained a better sense of time and culture. We had come to see history as a process and so valued the multicultural and historical understandings students brought to, and developed from, supportive school contexts. While differences in their experiences and ages led students to explore different issues and questions, they all grew through a consideration of new ideas and connections. Students realized that their opinions mattered, and as a result they became willing to share their ideas and thoughts with others. Inquiry became a valued part of their lives as they moved away from trying to find only answers and facts to searching for new questions and understandings in a continuous cycle of inquiry. As teacher researchers, we ended with new questions about inquiry and ways to support our students as they explore questions of significance in their lives and worlds.

Marni Schwartz

Holding Martin's Hand: Connecting to History Through Storytelling

MY WORK IN STORYTELLING TAKES ME ON MANY JOUR-
neys. I've traveled back in time to childhood memories, met the
ancients in myths and folktales, and in recent years walked the
roads of the deep South with a man I might have known during
my growing-up years, but didn't—Martin Luther King, Jr. By
sharing the story of this particular journey, I hope to invite
other teachers and students into learning by researching and
telling a tale.

Several years ago I was invited by the staff of an inner-city
school to do a biographical telling about Dr. King. I realized I
knew little about his life. I'd seen his name and photo in count-
less newspapers and heard rebroadcasts of his 1963 "I Have a
Dream" speech, but because I'd been a rather sheltered white
teenager living in a small upstate New York town in the 1960s, I
had little more than a vague awareness of the civil rights movement and the man so many claim as its leader. So I took the
school's offer, thinking of it as an assignment I needed to do.
What I discovered in that assignment was another journey, one
introducing me to far more than a man and a movement.

My Initial Search

At a local bookstore I found two King biographies for children,
Margaret Davidson's *I Have a Dream* (1968) and Dharathula H.
Millender's *Martin Luther King, Jr.—Young Man With a Dream*
(1983). In these I discovered stories of King's ancestry and boy-
hood. Within them I found the seeds of the seriousness, humor,
confusion, intelligence, oratory, and love that germinated as the
boy grew to manhood. Each bit of his history connected to another,
and Martin became a friend, a person whose story I had to know.

*Martin's paternal grandfather was an uneducated sharecropper trapped in a
system that kept him forever in debt. Martin's father, who had learned to
read and write, caught the landowner cheating his family out of earnings due
them, but was discouraged from making waves. Disillusioned, he eventually
left the plantation for Atlanta, looking for a better life. There he worked at
various jobs, attended night school, put himself through Morehouse College,
and became a preacher.*

*Martin's maternal grandfather had a different life. The Reverend Adam
Daniel Williams had been a preacher since 1894 in Atlanta and was known*

for his fiery sermons decrying segregation. A friend of W. E. B. DuBois,
Williams helped build the NAACP, which actively fought injustices toward
blacks. Reverend Williams believed strongly in the power of education to
transform lives. He sent his daughter Alberta to Spellman Seminary and
later to Hampton Institute in Virginia, where she became a teacher. Both
Alberta and her father saw something special in the ambitious young man
who came to preach at the Ebenezer Baptist Church. Reverend Williams took
him as an assistant, and Alberta chose him for her husband.

As I encountered these stories of Martin's ancestors, I began
to think of my own roots as a teacher and storyteller. My parents
and grandparents had been teachers and storytellers of a sort. In
different ways they modeled for me the way to listen to and
observe young learners and to draw out their natural curiosity
and enthusiasm. Taking that detour into my own ancestry
helped me develop a personal tale I called "Alive Alive Oh." I
used the Irish folksong about Molly Malone as the story's frame
because she plied the same trade as her parents. In the story I tell
how my Irish-American ancestors planted the seeds of teacher
and storyteller in me (Schwartz 1989). Similarly, in my students'
writings and comments I began to see more clearly the influence
of my early life experiences, how family members play a crucial
part in any child's learning. My sixth graders and I began to tell
the stories of people both in and outside our families whose
words and actions had touched our lives. Alissa described how
her brother's brain tumor had affected her entire family and
how proud she was of all he had accomplished despite his can-
cer. Matt told of Oscar, his dad's friend, who'd helped Matt learn
to tie his shoes by lending him his "giant" workboots with big
leather ties. In the telling Matt discovered other "Oscar memories," including the time he caught his first fish. Jason regaled us
with the story of his grandfather catching a baseball at Yankee
Stadium and being on a first-name basis with famous ballplay-
ers from "the olden days."

From Ancestry to Social History

Reading about the people and events that preceded Martin
Luther King's life awakened me, really for the first time, to how
his story was only part of a much larger story of change and

resistance to change. It was a concept my history books may have covered, but one my limited experience—and perhaps my teachers' methods—had kept me from understanding. I knew many of my students' lives were as sheltered as mine had been, and I hoped our talk, our sharing of tales, might open their minds to this bigger story.

Martin learned about segregation when he started school. He had to attend a different school from his white playmates, and their mothers made it clear the time for friendship was over. Once, young Martin and his father left a shoe store rather than move to seats in the back in order to be waited on. Another time Martin's father was addressed as "boy" by a policeman. His father corrected the officer, stating that his son was a boy but that he was a man.

Sharing these stories with my students, I was reminded of my own less hurtful but certainly memorable brushes with prejudice. I'd lost neighborhood friends by transferring to a newly built Catholic school at the beginning of third grade. Later, in high school, I'd heard that a boy's mother disapproved of me because of my Catholicism.

As I shared both Martin's and my stories, my students began to open up about the moments when they'd witnessed or felt the sting of stereotyping. One boy described his father's use of racial nicknames such as "jungle bunny" when referring to a black athlete. He said he knew his father talked like that only to show off for his friends. A Jewish child admitted that he wished more people understood the holidays he celebrated the way everyone knew about Christian holidays. Stories surfaced about feeling different simply because of clothing or talent or newness to a community or an organization. Everyone had experienced a feeling of separateness in some way. Martin's story was now our story, and we realized that, like him, we have a responsibility to speak out about prejudice in both its blatant and its subtle forms. No news broadcast or history lesson had ever brought me as close to Dr. King and his work as these children's simple stories and my own reflections on his life.

Martin often conversed with his mother about the history of his people. He regularly heard stirring speeches from his father's pulpit and participated in dinner-table debates about politics. He watched as the elder King participated in protests. He grew up with a fervor for the true emancipation his people had been promised by President Lincoln. In school Martin got to practice his own oratorical skills. He recited speeches such as Patrick Henry's "Give me liberty or give me death," and he researched the story of his namesake, Martin Luther, discovering that Luther was also a preacher known for his resistance to the status quo.

From History to Literature ❚

As I began to choose moments from Martin's childhood experiences to include in my telling, I was surprised and delighted to come across the young man's interest in Langston Hughes. Millender's book briefly describes the day Hughes visited King's class at Oglethorpe Elementary, the campus school of Atlanta University.

The enthusiastic boy even danced the Charleston as he recited "Negro Dancers" for its author. During the visit Martin also got to hear Hughes read "I, Too," a poem about the hope that black people would gain equality in America.

This image of the poet-teacher helping children find the literature that will both delight and enlighten them continues to guide my work as teacher and storyteller.

I already had some knowledge of Langston Hughes from my days as a college English major. I'd struggled to make sense of much of the literature assigned by my professors, but I found Hughes's poems to be more accessible. When I became a teacher I purchased a recording of Hughes's poems read by actors Ruby Dee and Ossie Davis (Hughes 1969). Their performances brought life to Hughes's musical rhythms and offered me layers of meaning I hadn't seen before. I hadn't played the record in a while, so I dug it out. Even scratches and skips didn't keep my students from enjoying Ruby Dee's feisty "Madam and Her Madam" and "Madam and the Rent Man." Such poems started us talking about what we knew of poverty and economic struggle. Few of us knew poverty personally, but by re-telling the stories we'd seen in movies and read in books or heard from grandparents, we began to raise our awareness.

Digging into Langston Hughes's life and work led me to more current authors whose writings would give me and my students a closer connection to black history. I'd encountered Alice Walker's writings first in the pages of *Ms.* magazine. Now I wanted to search out more of her prose and poetry. Together my students and I found Gwendolyn Brooks, Nikki Giovanni, Eloise Greenfield, and a host of other poets. We found the fiction and nonfiction of Julius Lester and Virginia Hamilton. Going through old college books I discovered ones I'd only sampled previously: *Black Voices* edited by Abraham Chapman (1968), *Soulscript* compiled by June Jordan (1970), and *My Name Is Black*, collected by Amanda Ambrose (1973). Chapman's collection contained the prose and poetry of Langston Hughes's contemporaries, the writings of friends of Martin Luther King, Jr., and works by younger, more radical writers who had broken away from King's philosophy of nonviolence. Every literary path led me to yet another.

Returning to Martin's life, I found his experiences with higher education fascinating. College for me had been disappointing academically; I had learned more during rathskeller conversations than class lectures.

Morehouse College, all black and all male, "offered King the academic freedom to discuss the evils of segregation openly" (Schulke and McPhee 1986). King studied sociology and continued to develop his oratorical skills. At first he rejected the idea of the ministry as unintellectual and hoped to make social change in another field, perhaps the law. One summer he took a job in Connecticut and found that he and his friends could go to theaters, stores, and restaurants freely. Those experiences furthered his desire to see laws change in the South.

His college years offered Martin a series of mentors. The sermons and lectures of Dr. Benjamin Mays, the president of Morehouse, and those of speakers he brought to the college had a profound influence on Martin. Many professors "taught a 'social gospel' that Martin found intellectually stimulating and socially relevant" (Schulke and McPhee 1986). It was at Morehouse that he first read the Henry David Thoreau essay "Civil Disobedience." By the time he was a junior, Martin had dropped the idea of law because he'd come to see that "the ministry could be intellectually meaningful as well as emotionally inspiring. He began to see, too, that the pulpit was the most direct route to his people" (Schulke and McPhee 1986).

At Crozer Theological Seminary in Pennsylvania Martin was introduced to the ideas of Mahatma Gandhi by a few teachers, but was especially

drawn to the ideal of nonviolence by a powerful lecturer, Dr. Mordecai John-
son, president of Howard University, who had traveled to India to study the
life and work of the Indian social philosopher. Martin was fascinated by what
Gandhi had accomplished through passive resistance. His teachers, readings,
and further studies in a doctoral program at Boston University contributed
to Martin's growth as a thinker and speaker.

In May 1954 Martin preached his first sermon in Montgomery. That
was the same month the U. S. Supreme Court ordered all schools desegre-
gated in the famous decision, Brown vs. Board of Education.

As I read about and connected the events in Martin Luther
King's life with the events shaping what came to be called the
civil rights era, my favorite story was that of Montgomery's
bus boycott. Rosa Parks's refusal to give up her seat was the
spark that lit the brush Montgomery's black leaders had been
gathering.

Jo Ann Robinson, a leader in the Women's Political Council, suggested it
was time for a bus boycott. Everyone agreed to endorse the one-day boycott
on Monday, December 5. That morning Martin and Coretta King watched
from their window as each bus passed with not a single black occupant. That
afternoon the boycott leaders met, formed the Montgomery Improvement
Association, and elected King as its leader. A citywide meeting held that
evening for the purpose of discussing the future of the boycott was Martin's
debut on the stage of struggle he would come to know well. "There comes a
time," he said again and again that night to the thousands who were listen-
ing and, for the first time perhaps, believing in the possibility of change.

King's story thereafter included marches, confrontations,
bombings and other threats, arrests, speeches, and meetings
with legislators and presidents. I found myself often side-
tracked from his personal story to the events connected to the
greater movement: the passing of laws, the arrests of individuals, the focus on whites such as George Wallace and Bull Con-
nors who strongly opposed integration. I made a time line of
events and stories so I could keep the progression straight in
my mind. I'd never seen so clearly how small and big events are
intertwined in history, how one person's actions can affect an
entire nation if the time is right.

My Journey Continues

In my search to find out more I ordered *Free at Last—A History of the Civil Rights Movement and Those Who Died in the Struggle* (Bullard 1990). This publication provides photos and stories of people, both black and white, who were lynched for crimes they didn't commit, killed for helping register black voters, beaten or trampled during riots, or assassinated for their role in trying to get laws changed. The Southern Poverty Law Center, which published it, produces and distributes free to educators a series of guides called *Teaching Tolerance*. Reading such material and sharing it with my students not only offered us a look at the past but also made us aware of the "small" injustices around us in our classroom, our school, and our community. We began to notice instances of racial and ethnic hatred still being reported around our nation and the world. As the year progressed the themes of intolerance and acceptance both in everyday life and in the events of history began to turn up in students' writings and discussions. Not every middle schooler caught my enthusiasm. Some watched my ongoing quest for understanding with a mixture of awe and amusement. Noting how many drafts I made for the civil rights time line, one student asked, "You're doin' this just for *yourself*?" I laughed and assured him someday he'd find an issue or a person worthy of independent study.

When it finally came time to tell Martin's story, I was nervous. Overwhelmed by all I'd learned, I could hear the echo of my own early schoolteachers' voices warning, "Limit your topic." On the two-hour drive down the thruway to Newburgh's Gardnertown Fundamental Magnet School I mentally reviewed the outline of events I wanted to include. However, I still lacked a focus, a thread that would connect the bits of story as I told them. Then I walked into the school and was greeted by children wearing t-shirts on which they had drawn their dreams. Like Martin, they believed in the future and were making plans to take their place in it. And so I began, "Just like you, young Martin Luther King was a child with a dream . . ."

Works Cited

ADULT WORKS

Atwell, N. 1987. *In the middle: Writing, reading, and learning with adolescents.* Portsmouth, NH: Boynton/Cook-Heinemann.

Banks, J. A. 1975. *Teaching strategies for ethnic studies.* Boston: Allyn and Bacon.

Bath, S. R. 1992. Trade-book minigroups: A cooperative approach to literature. *The Reading Teacher* 46:3 (November).

Broadhead, R., and L. Burnett. 1955. Areas of change and controversy. In R. Ellsworth and O. Sand, eds., *Improving the social studies curriculum: Twenty-sixth yearbook of the National Council for the Social Studies.* Menasha, WI: George Banta Publishing Co.

Bullard, S. 1990. *Free at last: A history of the civil rights movement and those who died in the struggle.* Montgomery, AL: The Southern Poverty Law Center.

Burke, C. 1992. Class presentation at the University of Arizona.

Calkins, L. 1991. *Living between the lines.* Portsmouth, NH: Heinemann.

Cambourne, B. 1988. *The whole story: Natural learning and the acquisition of literacy in the classroom.* Auckland: Ashton Scholastic.

Campbell, R. 1990. *Reading together.* Buckingham: Open University Press.

Chapman, A, ed. 1968. *Black voices: An anthology of Afro-American Literature.* New York: New American Library.

203

Cohen, J. 1993. Constructing race in an urban high school: In their minds, their mouths, their hearts. In L. Weis and M. Fine, *Beyond silenced voices: Class, race, and gender in US schools*. New York: State University of New York Press.

Cummins, J. 1993. Empowering minority students: A framework for intervention. In L. Weis and M. Fine, *Beyond silenced voices: Class, race, and gender in US schools*. New York: State University of New York Press.

Davis, O. L., Jr. 1981. Understanding the history of the social studies. In H. D. Mehlinger and O. L. Davis, Jr., eds., *The social studies: Eightieth yearbook of the National Society for the Study of Education*. Chicago: University of Chicago.

Edelsky, C., B. Altwerger, and B. Flores. 1991. *Whole language: What's the difference?* Portsmouth, NH: Heinemann.

Eisner, B. 1988. *Children and play in the Holocaust: Games among the shadows*. Amherst: University of Massachusetts Press.

Elkind, D. 1989a. Developmentally appropriate practice: Philosophical and practical implications. *Phi Delta Kappan* (October): 113–117.

———. 1989b. *Teachers as mediators*. Beaverton School District, Staff Development Presentation, Beaverton, OR. November.

Fifield, K. *The Scottish storyline method*. Presentation of Educational Resources Northwest, Portland, OR. May.

Fisher, P. 1990. Teaching the essential skills through fine arts integration. *Theatre*. Tucson, AZ: Tucson/Pima Arts Council.

Freeman, Y. S., and S. D. Nofziger, Jr. 1991. WalkM to RnM 33: Vien vinidos al cualTo 33. In Y. M. Goodman, W. J. Hood, and K. S. Goodman, eds., *Organizing for whole language*. Portsmouth, NH: Heinemann.

Freire, P. 1972. *Pedagogy of the oppressed*. New York: Herder and Herder.

———. 1985. *The politics of education*. New York: Bergin & Garvey.

Galda, L. 1988. Readers, texts, and contexts: a response-based view of literature in the classroom. *New Advocate* 1: 92–102.

Goldstein, H., and M. Goldstein. 1980. *Reasoning ability of mildly retarded learners*. Reston, VA: The Council for Exceptional Children.

Goodman, K. 1986. *What's whole in whole language?* Portsmouth, NH: Heinemann.

Greenow, L. L., F. Ainsley, Jr., and G. S. Elbow. 1993. *People in time and place: World geography.* Morristown, NJ: Silver Burdett Ginn.

Harste, J. C., and K. G. Short, with C. Burke. 1988. *Creating classrooms for authors.* Portsmouth, NH: Heinemann.

Howells, R. F. 1992. Thinking in the morning, thinking in the evening, thinking at suppertime . . . *Phi Delta Kappan* (November): 223–225.

Huck, C. 1987. To know the place for the first time. *The Best of the Bulletin,* 1: 69–71.

James, B. M. 1989. *Something to live for, something to reach for: Students of a native survival school.* Saskatoon, Sask.: Fifth House Publishers.

Jarolimek, J. 1981. The social studies: An overview. In H. D. Mehlinger and O. L. Davis, Jr., eds., *The social studies: Eightieth yearbook of the National Society for the Study of Education.* Chicago: University of Chicago.

Jones, S., and S. Berman. 1991. *Talking about war in the Persian Gulf.* Cambridge, MA: Educators for Social Responsibility.

Keirns, J. 1993. *Issues in implementing developmentally appropriate practices.* Gesell Institute presentation, Eugene, OR. April.

Kelly, E. 1955. Teaching current issues in the school. In R. Ellsworth and O. Sand, eds., *Improving the social studies curriculum: Twenty-sixth yearbook of the National Council for the Social Studies.* Menasha, WI: George Banta Publishing Co.

Kriesberg, S. 1993. The Constitution and democratic education: Practicing what we preach. *Democracy and Education:* 25–30.

Levstik, L., and C. Pappas. 1987. Exploring the development of historical understandings. *Journal of Research and Development in Education* 21(1): 1–15.

Littlefair, A. 1991. *Reading all types of writing.* Buckingham: Open University Press.

Morrissett, I. 1981. The needs of the future and the constraints of the past. In H. D. Mehlinger and O. L. Davis, Jr., eds., *The social studies: Eightieth yearbook of the National Society for the Study of Education.* Chicago: University of Chicago.

The Native Booklist. 1993. Saskatoon, Sask.: Fifth House Publishers.

Noddings, N. 1988. An ethic of caring and its implications for instructional arrangements. *Journal of Education* 96(2): 215–230.

Ochoa, A. 1981. The Education of social studies teachers. In H. D. Mehlinger and O. L. Davis, Jr., eds., *The social studies: Eightieth yearbook of the National Society for the Study of Education.* Chicago: University of Chicago.

Pascual Morán, A. 1989. Hostos: Precursor de la educación para la paz. Puerto Rico: Editorial Sonador.

Piaget, J. 1977. *The development of thought*. New York: Viking.

Rief, L. 1992. *Seeking diversity*. Portsmouth, NH: Heinemann.

Schulke, F., and P. O. McPhee. 1986. *King remembered*. New York: W. W. Norton & Co.

Schwartz, M. 1989. Alive alive oh. *Language Arts* 66: 733–735.

Shor, I. 1987. *Freire for the classroom: A sourcebook for laboratory teaching*. Portsmouth, NH: Boynton/Cook-Heinemann.

Short, K. 1993. Integrating curriculum through inquiry cycles. Paper presented at the Annual Convention of the International Reading Association, San Antonio, TX. April 27.

Short, K. and J. Armstrong. 1993. Moving toward inquiry: Integrating literature into the science curriculum. *The New Advocate* 6(3): 183–199.

Short, K., and C. Burke. 1991. *Creating curriculum: Teachers and students as a community of leaders*. Portsmouth, NH: Heinemann.

Short, K., K. Crawford, M. Ferguson, G. Kauffman, J. Laird, and J. Schroeder. 1992. A critical perspective on discovery and Columbus: Exploring children's historical and cultural understanding. *Journal of Navajo Education* 10(1): 6–16.

Short, K., and C. Klassen. 1993. Literature circles: Hearing children's voices. In B. Cullinan, ed., *Children's voices: Talk in the classroom*. Newark, DE: International Reading Association.

Sims, R. 1982. *Shadow and substance: Afro American experience in contemporary children's fiction*. Urbana, IL: National Council of Teachers of English.

Sizer, T. 1983. *Horace's compromise*. Boston: Houghton Mifflin.

Taylor, D. 1990. Teaching without testing. *English Education* 22(1): 4–74.

Teaching Tolerance. 1992. Vol. 1, no. 1. Montgomery, AL: The Southern Poverty Law Center.

Teale, W. H. 1984. Reading to young children: Its significance for literary development. In H. Goelman, A. A. Oberg, and F. Smith, eds., *Awakening to literacy*. Portsmouth, NH: Heinemann.

Trelease, J. 1989. *The new read-aloud handbook*. New York: Penguin Books.

Turnure, J. E. 1986. Instruction and cognitive development: Coordinating communication and cues. *Exceptional Children* 53(2): 109–117.

Watson, D., C. Burke, and J. Harste. 1989. *Inquiring voices.* New York: Scholastic.

Wichert, S. 1989. *Keeping the peace: Practicing cooperation and conflict resolution with preschoolers.* Philadelphia, PA: New Society Publishers.

Wigginton, E. 1985. *Sometimes a shining moment: The foxfire experience.* Garden City, NY: Anchor Press/Doubleday.

ADOLESCENT AND CHILDREN'S BOOKS

Aardema, V. 1991. *Borrequita and the coyote.* New York: Knopf.

Abells, C. B. 1983. *The children we remember.* New York: Kar-Ben Copies.

Ada, A. F. 1991. *The gold coin.* New York: Atheneum.

Adler, D. 1991. *A picture book of Christopher Columbus.* New York: Holiday.

Aliki. 1965. *A weed is a flower: The life of George Washington Carver.* New York: Prentice Hall.

———. 1976. *Corn is maize.* New York: HarperCollins.

Allen, P. 1980. *Mr. Archimedes' bath.* New York: Lothrop, Lee & Shepard.

Ambrose, A, ed. 1973. *My name is Black: An anthology of Black poets.* New York: Scholastic.

Andrews, J. 1985. *Very last first time.* New York: Atheneum.

———. 1991. *The auction.* New York: Macmillan.

Armstrong, J. 1985. *Slash.* Penticton, British Columbia: Theytus Books.

Armstrong, W. H. 1972. *Sounder.* New York: Harper Trophy.

Asimov, I. 1974. *How did we find out about germs?* New York: Avon.

Baker, J. 1987. *Where the forest meets the sea.* New York: Greenwillow.

———. 1991. *Window.* New York: Greenwillow.

Baldwin, M. 1981. *The boys who saved the children.* New York: J. Messner.

Barchas, S. 1975. *I was walking down the road.* New York: Scholastic.

Batherman, M. 1981. *Before Columbus.* New York: Houghton.

Beatty, P. 1984. *Turn homeward, Hannalee.* New York: William Morrow.

———. 1987. *Charley Skedaddle.* New York: William Morrow.

———. 1992. *Who comes with cannons?* New York: William Morrow.

Block, G., and M. Drucker. 1992. *Rescuers: Portraits of moral courage in the Holocaust.* New York: Holmes & Meier Publishers.

Bunting, E. 1980. *Terrible things.* New York: Harper & Row.

———, E. 1988. *How many days to America?* New York: Clarion.

———. 1992. *Summer wheels.* San Diego: Harcourt.

Buss, F. L. with D. Cubias. 1991. *Journey of the sparrows.* New York: Lodestar Books.

Byars, B. 1977. *The Pinballs.* New York: Scholastic.

Caduto, M., and J. Bruchac. 1989. *Keepers of the earth.* Golden, CO: Fulcrum.

Callaway, S., and G. Witherspoon. 1974. *Grandfather stories of the Navahos.* Rough Rock, AZ: Rough Rock Press.

Campbell, M. 1973. *Halfbreed.* Toronto: McClelland and Stewart.

Cartwright, S. 1976. *What's in a map?* New York: Coward, McCann & Geoghegan.

Chang, I. 1991. *A separate battle: Women and the Civil War.* New York: Lodestar.

Cherry, L. 1992. *A river ran wild.* San Diego: Harcourt.

Clapp, P. 1986. *The tamarack tree.* New York: Lothrop.

Climo, S. 1987. *A month of seven days.* New York: Harper-Collins/Crowell.

Cobb, V. 1972. *Sense of direction.* New York: Parent's Magazine Press.

Coerr, E. 1977. *Sadako and the thousand paper cranes.* New York: Putnam.

Collura, M. E. L. 1984. *Winners.* Saskatoon, Sask.: Western Producer Press.

Cormier, R. 1980. *8 plus 1.* New York: Bantam Books.

Crowder, J. 1986. *Tonibah and the rainbow.* Bernalillo, NM: Upper Strata Ink.

Culleton, B. 1983. *In search of April Raintree.* Winnipeg: Pemmican Press.

Davidson, M. 1968. *I have a dream: The story of Martin Luther King.* New York: Scholastic.

Dorris, M. 1992. *Morning girl.* New York: Hyperion.

Esbensen, B. 1992. *Who shrank my grandmother's house?* New York: Harper.

Evers, L. 1980. *The southwest corner of time: Hopi Navajo Papago Yaqui tribal literature.* Tucson: University of Arizona Press.

Evers, L., and F. Molina. 1987. *Yaqui deer songs Maso Bwikam: A native American poetry.* Tucson: SunTracks and the University of Arizona Press.

————. 1990. *WO'I Bwikam: Coyote songs*. Tucson: Chax Press.

Fischetto, L. 1991. *All pigs on deck*. New York: Delacorte.

Fisher, L. 1990. *Prince Henry the navigator*. New York: Macmillan.

Foreman, M. 1991. *The boy who sailed with Columbus*. New York: Archade.

Frank, A. 1952. *Anne Frank: The diary of a young girl*. New York: Simon & Schuster.

Friedman, I. 1984. *How my parents learned to eat*. Boston: Houghton Mifflin.

Fritz, J. 1982. *Homesick: My own story*. New York: Dell Publishers.

Gallaz, C., and R. Innocenti. 1985. *Rose Blanche*. Mankato, MN: Creative Education.

Garcia, M. 1986. *The adventures of Connie and Diego*. Emeryville, CA: Children's Book Press.

Garza, C. 1990. *Family pictures*. Emeryville, CA: Children's Book Press.

George, J. C. 1972. *Julie of the wolves*. New York: Harper and Row.

Gibbons, G. 1990. *How a house is built*. New York: Holiday.

Gilman, P. 1992. *Something from nothing*. New York: Scholastic.

Gleiter, J., and I. Thompson. 1985. *Christopher Columbus*. Nashville, TN: Ideals.

Goble, P. 1988. *Iktomi and the boulder*. New York: Orchard.

Greene, B. 1973. *Summer of my German soldier*. New York: Dial Press.

Hansen, J. 1986. *Which way freedom?* New York: Walker.

————. 1988. *Out from this place*. New York: Walker.

Hartman, G. 1991. *As the crow flies*. New York: Bradbury.

Haskins, J. 1991. *Outward dreams: Black inventors and their inventions*. New York: Walker.

Havill, J. 1986. *Jamaica's find*. New York: Scholastic.

Hayes, J. 1983. *Coyote &*. Santa Fe, NM: Mariposa.

Highway, T. 1988. *The Rez sisters*. Saskatoon, Sask.: Fifth House Publishers.

Hobbs, W. 1989. *Bearstone*. New York: Avon Books.

Howard, E. 1991. *Aunt Flossie's hats*. New York: Clarion.

Hubert, Cam. 1978. *Dreamspeaker*. New York: Avon Books.

Hunt, I. 1970. *No promises in the wind*. New York: Tempo Books.

Hutchins, P. 1968. *Rosie's walk*. New York: Macmillan.

Jacobs, F. 1992. *The Tainos*. New York: Putnam.

James, Becky. 1989. *Something to live for, something to reach for*. Saskatoon, Sask.: Fifth House Publishers.

Jeffers, S. 1991. *Brother Eagle, Sister Sky*. New York: Dial.

Jordan, J. 1970. *Soulscript: Afro-American Poetry*. Garden City, NY: Doubleday & Co.

Keegan, M. 1991. *Pueblo boy: growing up in two worlds*. New York: Cobblehill Books.

Kellogg, S. 1973. *Island of the Skog*. New York: Dial.

King, T., ed. 1990. *All my relations: An anthology of contemporary Canadian native fiction*. Toronto, McClelland and Stewart.

Knowlton, J. 1985. *Maps and globes*. New York: Crowell.

La Farge, O. 1929. *Laughing boy*. New York: New American Library.

Lattimore, D. 1987. *The flame of peace: A tale of the Aztecs*. New York: Harper.

Lauber, P. 1990. *Seeing earth from space*. New York: Macmillan.

Leon, G. 1989. *Explorers of the Americas before Columbus*. New York: Watts.

Lesley, C., ed. 1991. *Talking leaves: Contemporary Native American short stories*. New York: Bantam Doubleday Dell Publishing Group.

Lester, J. 1968. *To be a slave*. New York: Dial Press.

Liestman, V. 1991. *Columbus Day*. Minneapolis: Carolrhoda.

Locker, T. 1991. *The land of gray wolf*. New York: Dial.

Lopez, B. 1990. *Crow and Weasel*. San Francisco: North Point.

Lyon, G. E. 1988. *Borrowed children*. New York: Bantam Books.

Maestro, B., and G. Maestro. *The discovery of the Americas*. New York: Lothrop.

Martin, B., Jr., and J. Archambault. *Knots on a counting rope*. New York: The Trumpet Club.

Maruki, T. 1980. *Hiroshima no pika*. New York: Lothrop, Lee & Shepard.

Matthews, A. 1985. *Journey of Natty Gann*. New York: Pocket Books.

Matthews, R. 1991. *Eyewitness: Explorer*. New York: Knopf.

Mazer, H. 1986. *The cave under the city*. New York: Thomas Y. Crowell Junior Books.

McGill-Callahan, S. 1991. *And still the turtle watched*. New York: Dial.

McLarren, A. 1991. *Roxaboxen*. New York: Lothrop.

McSwigan, M. 1942. *Snow treasure*. New York: E. P. Dutton and Co.

Medearis, A. S. 1990. *Picking peas for a penny*. New York: Scholastic.

———. 1991. *Dancing with the Indians*. New York: Holiday House.

Meltzer, M. 1972. *Slavery II: From the Renaissance to today.* Chicago: Cowles Book Co.

———. 1976. *Never to forget: The Jews of the Holocaust.* New York: Harper & Row.

———. 1980. *All times, all peoples: a world history of slavery.* New York: HarperCollins.

———. 1988. *Rescue: The story of how Gentiles saved Jews in the Holocaust.* New York: Harper & Row.

Mendez, P. 1989. *The black snowman.* New York: Scholastic.

Merriam, E. 1991. *The wise woman and her secret.* New York: Simon & Schuster.

Merrill, J. 1992. *The girl who loved caterpillars.* New York: Philomel.

Millender, D. H. [1969] 1983. *Martin Luther King, Jr.: Young man with a dream.* New York: Aladdin.

Moore, L. 1987. *The ugly duckling.* New York: Scholastic.

Murphy, J. 1990. *The boys' war: Confederate and Union soldiers talk about the Civil War.* New York: Clarion.

Musgrove, M. 1976. *Ashanti to Zulu: African traditions.* New York: Dial Books for Young Readers.

Myers, W. D. 1991. *Now is your time: The African American struggle for freedom.* New York: HarperCollins.

Naylor, P. 1991. *Shiloh.* New York: Dell.

Near, H. 1993. *The great peace march.* New York: Henry Holt.

New Mexico People and Energy Collective. 1981. *Red ribbons for Emma.* Berkeley, CA: New Seed Press.

O'Dell, S. 1978. *Island of the blue dolphins.* New York: Dell.

Ortiz, S. 1977. *The people shall continue.* Emeryville, CA: Children's Book Press.

Parker, S. 1992. *Galileo and the universe.* New York: HarperCollins.

Paulson, T. 1990. *Jack and the beanstalk.* New York: Birch Lane.

Peck, R. N. 1972. *A day no pigs would die.* New York: Dell.

Pelta, K. 1991. *Discovering Christopher Columbus: How history is invented.* Minneapolis: Lerner.

Pitts, P. 1988. *Racing the sun.* New York: Avon Books.

Polacco, P. 1988. *The keeping quilt.* New York: Simon & Schuster.

———. 1992. *Mrs. Katz and Tush.* New York: Bantam.

Provensen, A., and M. Provensen. 1983. *The glorious flight across the channel with Louis Bleriot, July 25, 1909.* New York: Viking.

Quest Books. 1979. *Famous cities: London.* London: Chambers.

Ray, D. 1990. *A nation torn: The story of how the Civil War began.* New York: Lodestar.

Reeder, C. 1989. *Shades of gray.* New York: Avon.

Reimer, L., and W. Reimer. 1990. *Mathematicians are people, too.* Palo Alto, CA: Dale Seymour Publications.

Reiss, J. 1972. *The upstairs room.* New York: Crowell.

Richter, H. P. 1970. *Friedrich.* New York: Holt Rinehart and Winston.

Ride, S., and S. Oakie. 1987. *To space and back.* New York: Lothrop.

Robinson, M. 1990. *A woman of her tribe.* New York: Macmillan.

Rodanas, K. 1991. *Dragonfly's tale.* New York: Clarion.

Roessel, M. 1993. *Kinaaldá: A Navajo girl grows up.* Minneapolis: Lerner Publications.

Rogers, P. 1987. *From me to you.* New York: Orchard.

Rose, D. 1990. *The people who hugged the trees.* Niwot, CO: Roberts Rhinehart.

Ryan, P. 1990. *Explorers and mapmakers.* New York: Lodestar.

Rylant, C. 1987. *Birthday presents.* New York: Orchard.

———. 1992. *An angel for Solomon Singer.* New York: Orchard.

San Souci, R. D. 1989. *The talking eggs.* New York: Scholastic.

Savala, R. 1980. *Autobiography of a Yaqui poet.* Tucson: University of Arizona Press.

Sawyer, D. 1988. *Where the rivers meet.* Winnipeg: Pemican Publications.

Say, A. 1990. *El Chino.* New York: Houghton.

Scholes, K. 1989. *Peace begins with you.* Boston: Little, Brown.

Scieszka, J. 1989. *The true story of the three little pigs.* New York: Orchard.

Sharmat, M. 1980. *Gila monsters meet you at the airport.* New York: Aladdin.

Silverstein, S. 1964. *The giving tree.* New York: Harper.

Sis, P. 1991. *Follow the dream.* New York: Knopf.

Slipperjack, R. 1987. *Honour the sun.* Winnipeg: Pemican Publications.

———. 1992. *Silent words.* Saskatoon, Sask.: Fifth House Publishers.

Smucker, B. 1977. *Underground to Canada.* Toronto: Clarke.

———. 1985. *White Mist.* Toronto: Puffin Books.

Spier, P. 1980. *People.* New York: Doubleday.

Spinelli, J. 1990. *Maniac Magee.* New York: Scholastic.

Stanley, J. 1992. *Children of the dust bowl: The true story of the school at Weedpatch Camp.* New York: Trumpet Club.

Steele, W. O. 1958. *The perilous road*. New York: Scholastic.

Steinbeck, J. 1937. *Of mice and men*. New York: Bantam.

———. 1960. The origin of tularecito. In *The pastures of heaven*. New York: Viking Press.

———. 1967. Flight. Selected by P. Covici in *The portable Steinbeck*. New York: Viking Press.

Sullivan, G. 1990. *The day we walked on the moon*. New York: Scholastic.

Surat, M. 1983. *Angel child, dragon child*. New York: Scholastic.

Taylor, D. H. 1990. *Toronto at Dreamer's Rock*. Saskatoon, Sask.: Fifth House Publishers.

Taylor, M. 1976. *Roll of thunder, hear my cry*. New York: Bantam.

———. 1981. *Song of the trees*. New York: Bantam.

———. 1989. *The friendship and the gold Cadillac*. New York: Bantam-Skylark.

———. 1990. *Mississippi bridge*. New York: Bantam-Skylark.

Taylor, M. D. 1987. *The friendship*. New York: Dial.

Taylor, T. 1969. *The cay*. New York: Doubleday.

Tsuchiya, Y. 1988. *Faithful elephants: A true story of animals, people, and war*. Boston: Houghton Mifflin.

Turner, A. 1987. *Nettie's trip south*. New York: Macmillan.

Uchida, Y. 1981. *Jar of dreams*. New York: Atheneum.

Velie, A., ed. 1991. *The lightning within: An anthology of contemporary American Indian fiction*. Lincoln: University of Nebraska Press.

Waddell, M. 1990. *Grandma's Bill*. New York: Orchard.

Warner, L. S. 1993. *From slave to abolitionist: The life of William Wells Brown*. New York: Dial.

Weiss, H. 1991. *Maps: Getting from here to there*. New York: Houghton.

Wheatley, N., and D. Rawlins. 1992. *My place*. Brooklyn: Kane/Miller Book Publishers.

Wheeler, J. 1989. *Brothers in arms*. Winnipeg: Pemican Publications.

Wigginton, E. 1985. *Sometimes a shining moment*. Garden City, NY: Anchor Press/Doubleday.

Wild, M. 1991. *Let the celebrations begin*. New York: Orchard.

Williams, B. 1975. *Kevin's grandmother*. New York: Dutton.

Williams, J. 1976. *Everyone knows what a dragon looks like*. New York: Four Winds.

Williams, V. 1981. *Three days on a river in a red canoe*. New York: Mulberry.

Winter, J. 1988. *Follow the drinking gourd*. New York: Knopf.

Wolfe, A. 1988. *Earth elder stories*. Saskatoon, Sask.: Fifth House Publishers.

Yashima, T. 1955. *Crow boy*. New York: Viking.

Yolen, J. 1977. *The seeing stick*. New York: Crowell.

———. 1988. *The devil's arithmetic*. New York: Viking Kestral.

———. 1990. *Sky dogs*. San Diego: Harcourt.

———. 1992. *Encounter*. San Diego: Harcourt.

Yorinks, A. 1987. *Company's coming*. New York: Scholastic.

Young, E. 1992. *Seven blind mice*. New York: Philomel.

Yue, C., and D. Yue. 1992. *Christopher Columbus: How he did it*. New York: Houghton.

Zelinsky, P. 1986. *Rumpelstiltskin*. New York: Dutton.

Zolotow, C. 1972. *William's doll*. New York: Harper.

———. 1992. *This quiet lady*. New York: HarperCollins.

Audiovisual Materials

The great depression; 1929–1939. 1968. Filmstrip. Pleasantville, NY: Guidance Associates.

Harley, B. 1990. *I'm gonna let it shine: A gathering of voices for freedom*. Recording. Seekonk, MA: Round River Records.

Hughes, L. 1969. *The poetry of Langston Hughes read by Ruby Dee and Ossie Davis*. Recording. TCI 272. New York: Caedman.

The reckless years; 1919–1929. 1968. Filmstrip. Pleasantville, NY: Guidance Associates.

Venet, N., and B. Mize. 1963. The ballad of Momma Rosa Parks. On *This land is your land: Songs of racial justice*. Recording. Detroit: International Union, UAW.

Social Studies Resources

Charting a Course: Social Studies for the 21st Century. 1989. A Report of the Curriculum Task Force of the National Commission on Social Studies in the Schools.
Suggests content for social studies curriculum with history and geography at the center. Organized by grade-level groupings (K–3, 4–6, 7–8, 9–12). NCSS Publications, 3501 Newark St. NW, Washington, DC 20016.

Curriculum Standards for Social Studies. 1994. National Task Force for Social Studies Standards, Donald O. Scheider, Chair.
The conceptual components for social studies curriculum development as defined by the National Council for the Social Studies. Can be used as a reference for developing K–12 curriculum. NCSS Publications, 3501 Newark St. NW, Washington, DC 20016.

History/Social Science Framework. 1988. California State Department of Education.
The California framework emphasizes integrating literature into the history/social studies curriculum. Specific books, in a variety of genres, are suggested by topic area. California State Department of Education, Bureau of Publication Series, P.O. Box 271, Sacramento, CA 95802-0271.

K–6 Geography, Themes, Key Ideas and Learning Opportunities. National Council for Geographic Education.
Practical book for the teaching of geography. National Council for Geographic Education, 16A Leonard Hall, Indiana University of Pennsylvania, Indiana, PA 15705.

National Council for the Social Studies (NCSS).
National professional organization, with state and local chapters, for social studies educators. Membership benefits include *The Social Studies Professional*, a newsletter, and one of two journals, *Social Education* or *Social Studies and the Young Learner*. NCSS holds an annual national conference. National Council for the Social Studies, 3501 Newark St. NW, Washington, DC 20016.

Social Education.
Journal published seven times a year by the National Council for the Social Studies. Addresses the teaching of social studies at the elementary through university level. *Social Education*, 3501 Newark St. NW, Washington, DC 20016.

Social Studies and the Young Learner.
Journal published quarterly by the National Council for the Social Studies. Specifically for teachers of grades K–6. *Social Studies and the Young Learner*, 3501 Newark St. NW, Washington, DC 20016.

Social Studies School Service.
A distribution company that produces catalogs of social studies materials. Reviews of materials are written by teachers. Social Studies School Services, 10200 Jefferson Blvd., P.O. Box 802, Culver City, CA 90232-0802.